# THAT THEY
# MIGHT KNOW

*For dear friends
by Dot & Lefty*

by
**Richard Kruis**

*Richard Kruis*

Creative Designs, Inc.
Albuquerque, NM

Edited by Geoffrey F. Peek
Cover Design by Jonathan D. Dailey

Published by
Creative Designs, Inc.
11024 Montgomery NE, Suite 311
Albuquerque, New Mexico 87111
(505) 856-2600

ISBN 1-880047-32-2

# DEDICATION

To Mae, my beloved wife and co-laborer on the Indian Field. She stood by me through difficult and trying times while raising our large family. I couldn't have finished this script without her typing and editing.

# ACKNOWLEDGEMENTS

I also want to acknowledge my deep appreciation to the native interpreters who were my assistants and bore with me when I made many blunders getting acquainted with Indian culture and language. Four Johns come to mind: John Tso, John George, John Charles, and John Talley. There were others such as Jimmy Beleen, Geronimo Martin, and Samson Yazzie who was my first helper. Much of the success of bringing the Good News to their people depended on their faithful interpretation to people who often weren't receptive. Nevertheless, the Holy Spirit blessed our feeble efforts in bringing His precious Word.

I also want to express appreciation for my eight children's patience while living in difficult circumstances in going off to boarding school at Rehoboth. Although they enjoyed the country living amongst the Navajo people.

All praise to God and the Lord Jesus who has called and blessed abundantly!

**Pastor Richard and Mae Kruis
Married Agust 21, 1947
Everett, Washington**

## *About The Author*

**Richard Kruis**

Richard Kruis was born in a country home near Jamestown Michigan. He was raised with a family of 12 children. He graduated from high school in Byron Center, Michigan and then went to work at the General Motors plant in Grand Rapids, Michigan for a few years until he was called into the armed services for 4 1/2 years during World War II.

He worked for a short time at Rehoboth, New Mexico, where he cooked for the mission school and hospital. There he met Mae van Zwol. They were married and he went to school at Reformed Bible College in Grand Rapids, Michigan in preparation for missionary service. He spent 1 1/2 years as a neighborhood evangelist for the Creston Christian Reformed Church in Grand Rapids until he was called to serve on the Navajo Indian Field in New Mexico.

The Kruis' spent many challenging and interesting years bringing the gospel to their Navajo friends. They experienced many heart breaking times as well as joys and rich blessings. This book relates in an easy to read story their life with their children on the reservation. Their eight grown children also share with you their feelings about being Missionary kids in a different cultural environment.

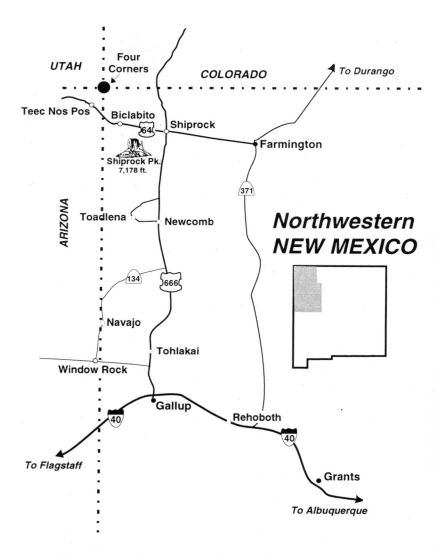

UTAH

Four Corners

COLORADO

To Durango

Teec Nos Pos

Biclabito

Shiprock

64

Farmington

Shiprock Pk. 7,178 ft.

371

ARIZONA

Toadlena

Newcomb

**Northwestern NEW MEXICO**

134

666

Navajo

Tohlakai

Window Rock

Gallup

Rehoboth

40

40

To Flagstaff

To Albuquerque

Grants

*The many locations shown in this map are mentioned in the text. The map is not to scale.*

# CONTENTS

**Chapter I**

# THAT THEY MIGHT KNOW

"*L*et's stop here." The words were no more than out of his mouth when the interpreter swerved the micro-bus off the rugged trail and pulled up under a gnarled old piñon tree. "This will give us shade, but watch out for the pitch on the rocks before you sit down this time", he said. He recalled how disturbed the missionary was the first time he sat in some sticky pitch which drips from the piñon tree during the hot summer months.

The two men were hungry after spending the morning calling on the Navajo in their hogans and summer shelters. They had been bringing the precious story of Jesus and His love.

Both men sat in silence for some time. Then John, the interpreter broke the silence with a question right out of the clear blue sky. "Rich, what made you decide to leave your home in Michigan to come way out here in our dry country to teach my people the Gospel?"

Missionary Richard Kruis continued to nibble on the mutton rib which the interpreter had shared out of his lunch. He was becoming quite an expert at picking the bone clean of its delicious meat as he had seen many a Navajo do. Was it because the meat was so good, so scarce, or because it was a pleasant past-time, or a combination of all three? At least one could have time to do some thinking and meditating in the process.

"That is a good question, John. Why does one leave his home and relatives to go to a strange people with a different culture to bring the Gospel? Perhaps we should ask ourselves that question more often. Why do we leave our homes and work to bring God's Word to other people? Why did you leave your work to bring the Gospel to your people? It is an important question, isn't it? It is strange that I was thinking along the same line when you broke into my thoughts, John. A quick answer would be that the Navajo might believe that Jesus is the Christ, the Son of God, and that believing they might have life through His name. That's it, in a nutshell. That they might believe that Jesus is the Christ, the Savior for all people, but I guess you wanted to know what led me, personally, to tell the Navajo this story.

"Have you noticed the little children playing in the sand down there near their hogan? It brings back memories of my childhood. They are constructing miniature hogans and sheep corrals. We made houses and farmyards. You see, I was brought up on a farm. I think those children do better than we did with their hands. Children are basically the same everywhere. These children are imitating the medicine man's ceremony with their little sand paintings. We built churches and sang hymns. I was thinking how in God's providence, I was raised in a Christian home and brought to church and Sunday School. It was in this early period of my life that a mission interest was implanted. I recall one of my first Sunday school lessons brought by my teacher. It was about the great Apostle Paul's missionary call to go to Macedonia to teach the heathen there that Jesus was the Christ. I can still hear her say in a most pleading way. `Come over to Macedonia and help us!' We never know when we teach little children what part of the lesson will be used or at what time the Holy Spirit will use what we teach.

When a missionary came to speak in one of our churches, if it wasn't too far, my folks went to hear him or her and took us children along. I recall how Miss Johanna Veenstra, our church's first missionary to Africa, pleaded for men to go to the dark continent. Later, Miss Veenstra's books came to our home and we were encouraged to read them. For me, it didn't take much encouragement because I thought they were most interesting. You know, John, if we want our children to become missionaries, we parents must show interest in missions and pray regularly for them in our homes.

"Life was not easy for us on the garden farm, for it meant long hours of hard work in the hot sun. It seemed to make the Lord's day so much more a day of rest and gladness. Mother encouraged us to read our Sunday School papers and study our catechism lessons on Sunday. I recall many times taking walks by myself to the wooded pasture in back of our farm, and there, I would spend time in prayer and meditation. These were days of sweet fellowship with the Lord and of dedication to Him. The idea of becoming a missionary to Africa never quite left my mind, but it never seemed very real either. The possibility that the Lord would use me for such a wonderful task seemed too good to be true. We had a large family and the possibility of getting a college education was very remote.

"But the Lord was leading and would direct my paths. As I look back, I can see how the Lord brought the many and varied experiences of life to place us finally on this field, so that the Navajo might know that Jesus is Savior. Would you like to hear some of the experiences? I will just hit the highlights because we have to go on. Maybe the Begays will be through with their lunch by then. I just saw their mother bring the children near the fire. I think they are having fried bread." John stretched out on the ground with a rock under his head for a pillow and said, "Tell me more, Rich."

"Well, John, I was telling you about being raised on the farm and not having much in the way of material things, but our life was a happy one. I had eleven brothers and sisters with whom to play. Our simple pastoral life makes me appreciate more the simple pastoral life of our Navajo people.

"After leaving high school, I went to work in a factory for a few years and then I was called into the Army. The call to be a missionary had faded for a time, but the Lord would use even this experience as a part of my training. It was in the service that I learned to take responsibility and had some valuable experiences in leadership. At the time the experience I had as a cook and mess sergeant seemed to be a useless one because I didn't figure on following this profession in civilian life. Now it comes in handy when we go out on overnight camping trips, or to help the family if Mae is sick.

"After spending four and a half years in the army, I went back to my job in the factory, but felt very restless. I considered going to college and seminary under the GI Bill of Rights. When I heard a stirring message from the pulpit or at a Bible Conference calling for young men and women to give their lives to spread the Gospel, I felt compelled to volunteer, but I wasn't prepared for such a high calling.

"Then something happened that changed the whole course of my life. It didn't just happen, for God was leading. A friend in our church saw an ad in our church paper asking for a man or woman to go to Rehoboth, New Mexico to

*That They Might Know*

cook for the Boarding school and Hospital. This ad was clipped out and sent by this friend with a note asking, "Wouldn't you be interested in this work?"' After prayerful consideration, I felt it was what the Lord wanted me to do. I wasn't married and it didn't look as if I would be. I had no family responsibilities, so I could take the cut in pay and this would be a service for the Lord on a mission field.

"I guess I told you before that I met Mae in 1947, at Rehoboth. Did I tell you she was from Washington State and I was from Michigan? The Lord directed our ways so our paths met here. She was a nurse at the hospital and I was the cook, so we saw each other every day and it wasn't long before we knew we were meant for each other, so we made plans to get married in Washington, where Mae's folks lived. Perhaps the "Land of Enchantment" had something to do with our own enchantment with each other. At least those were days of enchantment, and how fast they flew! They went by even faster than Jacob's seven years of waiting!

"It wasn't long before we both learned to love the Navajo people. I had gone out on several occasions on Sunday to substitute for a missionary to bring the Gospel. I also went a few times on camp work (home visiting). These experiences led us to the decision to go to the Reformed Bible Institute for further training with the hope of returning as missionaries to the Navajo people.

"We found out that the Navajo children like to tease as well as white children. The kids on detail in the kitchen or in the hospital kidded us every day after they knew we were dating. It was hard to leave these children for three years of schooling. It turned out to be four and a half years because there wasn't an opening on the Indian Field when I graduated from RBI.

"The years at RBI were years of spiritual growth as well as years of self discipline and an increase in the knowledge of God's Word. Perhaps the Lord will open the way for you to go to RBI some day, John. Pray about it. [John attended RBI later on.]

"As I said, the way was not open for us to return to the Indian Field when we got out of school. It was a disappointment, but the Secretary of our Mission Board, Dr. DeKorne, assured us that in time, the way would be open. The Lord directed us to do parish evangelism in Creston Christian Reformed Church in Grand Rapids, Michigan. This was also a valuable experience as a part of our preparation for further Kingdom work. While in this church and in our practical work while in school, we acquired many loyal Christian friends who have been a great source of strength and encouragement throughout the years of our service.

**Chapter II**

# AN EXCITING BEGINNING

As much as we enjoyed our time in Parish Evangelism, you don't know how excited we were when the Secretary of Missions called us and said we had the appointment to go to Shiprock, New Mexico. The Lord had opened the door for us to return to the Navajo Field! We did wait a week or ten days to give our answer to the Mission Board because we wanted to prayerfully consider the work we were doing at the time. Grand Rapids was also the Lord's vineyard and there were many white people who didn't know Jesus Christ.

The Creston Church gave us a warm farewell with the assurance that their prayers would go with us. It was going to be hard to say good-bye to loved ones at home, but it was also a wonderful feeling to be strengthened by the words and prayers of Christians.

It was in the last week of January, 1952, that we left for the Mission field. Mae hadn't seen her parents in Washington State for some time and they were anxious to see their grandchildren. The youngest, Trudy, was only 2 months old. I also had a brother doing mission work in Alberta, Canada. We decided to put some money with what the Board was paying for our transportation to New Mexico, to go a little farther to see my brother's family and Mae's relatives. That was quite a trip, John. The pioneers didn't have much over on us. At least that was the way we felt by the time we arrived in New Mexico. Some students from

New Mexico drove our car back to New Mexico for us. We traveled by train and because it was winter, we had to pack plenty of clothes, blankets and diapers. In the first night out of Chicago, the train was stalled two hours because of deep snow. We never realized how far West actually was!

Again, we were strengthened in spirit as we were sent on our way with the assurance that our Christian friends and relatives would be praying for us and the Navajo people.

How happy we were when the Santa Fe train finally came to a grinding halt at the Gallup depot. Friends from Rehoboth were at the station to greet us. Oh, how good it was to see the familiar Rehoboth buildings and the beautiful red rocks in the surrounding area! It seemed too good to be true. The Lord had brought us back here! We were greeted warmly by Rehoboth friends and asked to stay overnight before travelling the 100 miles to Shiprock. We knew Rev. Vander Stoep was expecting us and there was much to do up there, so we decided to go on the same day. We were anxious to get settled in our new home, too. But our plans were suddenly changed. While Mae was in the hospital renewing friendships and getting acquainted with new members of the hospital staff, I was out in front visiting with one of the missionaries.

Rick, our oldest son, was just two years old at the time, and thought the wall in front of the hospital was interesting to climb. Climbing was his favorite pastime. Just when my back was turned, he tumbled off the wall falling on his head. He was 'out' for just a short time and then began vomiting and twitching the muscles in one of his arms. We decided we had better have Dr. Bos see him and he decided we had better stay at Rehoboth over night so he could be observed. It turned out that he had a slight brain concussion, which brought on convulsions when he was injured or became suddenly excited. The doctor said he would outgrow them, but it was a matter of concern for several years...especially when the seizures occurred.

You can imagine how excited we were the next day when we had finished the 100 mile trip to Shiprock. First, we drove into Rev. Vander Stoep's yard and asked where our new home was. After a friendly greeting we drove about a half mile east to the "Castle on the hill". The large cement block house stood out in bold relief against the bright blue sky. We were a little concerned about the sudden drop off in front of the house, knowing the children would like to get as close as they could or try to use it as a slide. However, nothing bad ever happened.

The house had recently been attractively remodeled and made very comfortable. It wasn't long before we were settled and ready to go to work.

**Kruis first home in Shiprock**

Rev. Vander Stoep asked me to go with him and his interpreter to get acquainted with the field and type of work. I recall my first trip to Carisso Station (later called Teec Nos Pos) which was 32 miles west of Shiprock, just across the Arizona border. I thought we would never get there. The 32 miles seemed like 60, as we wound around curve after curve, over hills and through deep arroyos. Coming up a steep grade, Rev. Vander Stoep remarked, "Watch out, this blue clay hill is nasty when it is wet. This is where Dr. De Korne got stuck and had to stay overnight a few years ago." I thought that if this was going to be a part of my area of work, then it looked as if there will be few dull days ahead.

He warned about going through arroyos during a storm because the sudden cloud bursts out here could fill an arroyo with a wall of muddy water before you could get out and you could suddenly be washed down stream. One of his interpreters had lost a car that way in one of these arroyos. He had vacated his car just in time. It looked as if life would be more than exciting.

"Don't get discouraged," Samson, the interpreter, piped in, "the road isn't always this rocky. Sometimes we get a foot or two of snow, and then it's kind of hard to find the road. Of course, if you get stuck you can usually get a Navajo man to come with his horse and pull you out. That is, if he can find his horse."

A short time later, Samson and I had to go to the Government Boarding School at Aneth, Utah, to bring a Bible story to the primary grades there. I looked forward to this trip because it was the farthest northwestern point of our whole Indian Field. We even had to go into three states to get there - New Mexico, Colorado, and Utah. We cut across the southwestern tip of Colorado and the southeastern tip of

Utah where the Ute Indians lived. However, the Southern tip of Utah is Navajo reservation.

We packed our lunches so we could bring the Gospel to some Navajo camps along the way. Our class didn't start until three o'clock. I hadn't visited very many homes yet, so it turned out to be an eventful day.

A few miles out of Shiprock, we got a good view of beautiful Ute Mountain and beyond. We could see the snow covered peaks of the Rockies way off in the horizon. I was enjoying the fantastic scenery while traveling to work. Others traveled miles to see this! Suddenly, Samson said, "Look, there lies an elephant out in the field." I retorted, "Quit kidding, Sam. How dumb do you think I am?" He slowed the pickup down almost to a stop. "You can't see it if we get too close." Pointing to a huge yellowish mound of clay, the base of which was a dull gray, he described the head with its trunk and then the rest of the body. Sure enough, there it was, as big as could be and a good replica. From then on, whenever we travelled this way to Cortez with the family, the elephant was one of the landmarks to watch for.

As we neared Cortez, we came upon Chimney Rock, which was a huge pillar of rock rising abruptly from the plain at the foot of a great mesa. We later learned that the mesa was the back end of the famous Mesa Verde National Park, which could be entered ten miles East of Cortez.

As we turned west off the highway, we had a better view of Ute Mountain. Sam said "See the Ute Indian." I felt dumb because I looked everywhere around but saw no one. Maybe he blended in with the background like the Navajo hogans, which were so hard to find at first. Then my friend, pointing to the mountain, showed me how the mountain looked very much like a person lying on his back with his head several miles to the North and in the center his huge stomach, and at the end his bare toes, which were pillars of rock, sticking up out of the green pinon and pine trees.

We stopped briefly at the quaint trading post in the little Ute town of Towac at the foot of the mountain. I felt a little scared as we passed a group of Utes sitting in a circle, some with colorful blankets draped over their shoulders and wearing big western hats. They were gambling with playing cards such as the white man uses. They eyed us suspiciously as we passed. Others in the trading post didn't look too friendly either.

Samson asked for the mail for the school teachers and trader at Aneth. The postmaster (trader) said no one had been by for a few days, so there was quite a stack of mail. When we got in the pickup, Samson examined one of the packages more closely and scowled. I asked what was wrong. He said, "This is peyote. It's no good for our people. I really don't like to take it along."" I didn't know what peyote was and didn't think it was wise to ask too much at the time. Samson would say more after he knew me better and I had gained his confidence. I was to later experience in a very real and tragic way what Sam meant when he said, "It is not good for our people." I was to learn more about it even before the sun would set this very day.

As we were pulling away from the trading post, an elderly Navajo woman asked where we were going. We told her we were going toward the Aneth School. She asked if she could go along because her hogan was a short distance off the road. She said, "T'ah," (or, wait) and disappeared into the store. I was admiring the way her shiny black hair had been neatly folded at the back of her head and wound

*That They Might Know*

tightly with a bright green skein of yarn. Later, she reappeared with four little children and two older boys. The older boys were carrying a huge armful of bedding and the lady had her arms full of groceries. They all climbed into the back of the pickup with their belongings except the oldest boy who went back into the trading post and came out with a 50 pound sack of flour. I thought the woman had asked for a ride, but maybe she asked if we could move her family.

We bumped along over the twisting road which still bore the marks of winter. I don't know how Sam managed to stay on the narrow paths straddling the deep ruts. I held my breath as we plowed through some of the mud holes.

We figured we would bring our riders to their home and bring them the Gospel. After going about 12 miles we heard a tap on the cab window. One of the boys motioned for us to turn left. The "little ways off the road" seemed to never end. Finally, we came to several hogans nestled in the shadows of the rugged rocks. A well built sheep corral up against the wall of rock contained a large flock of sheep

**Hogan & mesa at Tótsosie (slim water)**

and goats. After the people, had unloaded their belongings, we asked if we could come in and bring God's Word to them. They looked a little puzzled. Perhaps they didn't know what we meant by "God's Word". They opened the door and we walked in. I was surprised how light the room was, seeing there were no windows, but all the light and fresh air had to come in through the hole in the dome of the round log home.

I wondered, at first, if we were going to sit or stand because I didn't see any chairs or other furniture in the room. With a friendly smile the woman brought a wood box and a small stool for us to sit on. She folded a pretty many colored Navajo blanket and laid it on the box. It made us feel welcome. We sat for what seemed a long time without saying a word. I felt uncomfortable not knowing what to say or when. After a while, Samson began talking in Navajo. Then he told me to go ahead. They wanted to hear the story. I spoke and Samson interpreted. We mentioned that we were new in their country and enjoyed the enchanting scenery but not the rough roads, if you could call them roads. They chuckled a little. Then we went on to tell them how all this beautiful country spoke of a great God who created them by His power and wisdom. The good things we have spoke of His love for us. We told them we would like to come back and tell them more from this Holy Word, which speaks of God's son, Jesus Christ.

We arose and shook hands. They said, "Thank you. Come again and tell us more." We praised God for this open door. We looked forward to returning to get better acquainted with those friendly people. We found that most Navajo are hospitable and friendly.

## Chapter III

# MY FIRST CONTACT WITH
# THE PEYOTE RELIGION

A s we continued on our way, we bumped along in silence for some time. Suddenly, a gray, scrawny coyote scampered across our path. Sam said, "I wish I had my deer rifle. At least I could give him a good scare. Speaking of scares," Sam added, "Did you know that a few years ago if a coyote ran in front of me, I would be plenty scared. Our superstitious ways wouldn't allow me to continue on my way. I would return back for fear that something tragic might happen."

After watching the slinking coyote for some time, we noticed in the distance, a small gray object weaving in and out of the sagebrush. Sam said, "That coyote must be awful hungry to be wasting so much time on that scrawny jackrabbit." We wondered who would win the race.

Speaking of getting a meal reminded us that it was about time to eat our lunch. We drove on until we got back on the trail to Aneth. We soon came upon a mound of rocks and decided to park. After asking the Lord's blessing on our food, we sat in quietness for a while. The silence was soon broken by a cheerful tinkling sound of bells and then a few goats and sheep appeared among the jagged rocks. It wasn't long before a little shepherd boy was seen jumping from rock to rock. When he spied our truck nearby, he dropped quickly behind a rock and we didn't see him again. I wished he would come out so we could get acquainted.

Samson said, "He must come from a very poor family. He is bare footed. It is hard on your feet to go barefoot in our country, because so many of the plants have sharp prickers and thorns. When you are chasing a stray sheep or goat you may get your feet full of cactus thorns or bull weeds." I believe God created these desert plants with prickers because there aren't many green things in arid lands.

Samson said, "There is a small hogan built into the side of a dark clay mound just a short ways away, perhaps the boy comes from that home. Shall we go and visit it?" I agreed to go. We parked the pickup a short ways away from the home and as we walked toward the home we heard some rhythmic sounds from that direction. I said, "It must be a gasoline washing machine." Samson replied, "No, I believe it is a peyote priest practicing on his drums." This made my heart beat a little faster as we neared the home because I had never seen a peyote priest before. I wondered, with a little fear, what the man's reaction would be when we came in with the Bible. I uttered a silent prayer.

After knocking on the door several times, he finally opened it. We greeted him with the usual "Ya'a'teh" and a hand shake. After a period of silence, Samson told him who we were and where we had come from. They both exchanged questions as to their clans. This is a very common question as Navajo meet for the first time. It's something like our Dutch custom to ask a new acquaintance if he or she knows so and so whom we know. I would often tell them that I am born for the wooden shoe clan, which always produces a good chuckle.

We were seated on a steel cot which stood against the log wall. We continued to talk of every day matters for a while, such as the need for rain and better grazing conditions or tribal affairs.

We then were ready to bring the gospel message telling about God, the Creator, and His Son the Good Shepherd. Every now and then he would utter an "mm" as if he understood or agreed. While Samson interpreted the message, I slyly glanced around the room and noticed how few furnishings and little food there was. It looked like a very poor home. I also noticed a long, narrow, highly polished box high up on one of the cross beams. [Later I was to learn that these boxes contained the peyote worshipper's feathers and rattles. These rattles are made of a hollowed out dry gourd and painted ornamentally. The handle was a beaded dowel of many bright colors and had feathers attached to the end.]

Before we left, the little shepherd boy we had seen, slipped through the crude wood door, glanced at us, and took a drink from the dipper setting in a water bucket on a small homemade table. The man muttered something to the boy and he hurried out again. We thanked the man for letting us come in and told him we would be back.

When we got back to the truck, Samson explained a little more about the peyote religion which was beginning to spread among the Navajo. Peyote, itself, is a dried fruit of a cactus plant usually grown in Texas and Mexico and mailed to leaders on the reservation. The use of it was outlawed at that time. The dried fruit, which has a somewhat salty taste and looks like a dried apricot, is eaten in its dried form or made into a stew. It is generally used at a "peyote church" ceremony.

This church is known as the Native American Church. The people sit in a circle in a home around a smoldering fire. A cigarette is lit and passed around to the adherents. Songs which may be Christian hymns or Navajo chants are sung. Prayers are said which are much like Christian prayers. During the ceremony people look at pictures of Jesus, Mary and the Crucifix. When peyote is eaten the person receives visions, usually of something to which his or her attention is given at the time. These visions are claimed to be the working of the Holy Spirit and people often claim they see Jesus personally. Because of the hallucinations and Christian symbols, peyote users claim to be Christian and they are seeking legalization for the use of peyote on the basis of it being a religious sacrament. The users claim it also has great healing powers. [Peyote was later legalized.]

The use of this herb has been known to bring injury to its users because, at times, some may become violent and not clearly know what they are doing or saying while under its use. An article taken from the Gallup Independent newspaper written by Mr. Don Lallin is attached. It is from the San Francisco Chronicle.

---

## PSYCHEDELIC SACRAMENT
*"Peyote pope" says feds ignore positive social value*

By Don Lattin
   The San Francisco Chronicle
   ANETH, Navajo Nation (Utah)— Peyote priest Emerson Jackson sprinkled some water on a handful of powdered cactus and molded the bitter potion into two balls about the size of strawberries.

   "This is a sacrament," said Jackson, handing the psychedelic mixture to Terrance Tom, a young Navajo man sponsoring an all-night peyote prayer meeting for 20 local members of the Native American Church.

   Everyone inside the giant tepee— erected earlier that day on a high bluff in the southeast corner of Utah —had already ingested two or three table-spoons of dried peyote, washing the gritty power down with an equally bitter peyote tea.

   Some time after midnight, the Navajos' peyote fans — kaleidoscopes of bright feathers and intricate bead work—took on a pulsing luminescence.

   American Indian chants, sung to the accompaniment of gourd rattles and a drum, carried the congregation off to another reality.

Chief Peyote, as the Indians call the psychedelic cactus button that fuels these ancient rites, was working its magic.

Ten years after the legality of these peyote ceremonies was supposedly ensured by the American Indian Religious Freedom Act, peyotists again find themselves in court.

In October, the U.S. Supreme Court will hear arguments in a lawsuit involving two members of the Native American Church in Oregon who were fired from their jobs at a drug treatment center for participating in an all-night peyote ritual.

Another lawsuit has been filed in federal court in Fresno, Calif., by a woman who was denied employment as a prison guard for admitting that she took peyote in church ceremonies.

Jackson, president of the Native American Church of North America and self-described "peyote pope," said both cases stem from the government's refusal to appreciate the positive social value and deep religious meaning of these traditional Indian rites.

"Catholics don't take wine at communion to get drunk, but to experience almighty God," Jackson said. "That's our purpose—to get into communion with the Holy Spirit."

To illustrate his point, Jackson invited a reporter to participate in a recent Saturday night peyote ritual not far from the Four Corners Monument, the only point in the United States common to four state borders.

The emotional, 11-hour ceremony began around 10 p.m., and it was a unique, powerful experience—a rare glimpse at the social, spiritual and psychedelic world of the Native American Church's Half Moon Ceremony.

The gatherings are usually held with a particular purpose—to pray for a sick child or help a church member work through a life crisis.

Terrance Tom's family sponsored and paid for the Saturday night session to pray for success in a new job that was taking Tom, his wife and his three young children off the reservation and into the white man's world in Albuquerque.

Members of the congregation, sitting inside the perimeter of the tepee, begin the ceremony by rolling their own cigarettes in pieces of dried corn husk, smoking the tobacco as a ritual act of purification, the way Catholic priests use incense before Mass.

Most of the night is spent passing a drum, gourd rattle and peyote staff around for spirited singing, drumming and chanting of the sect's guttural, fast-paced hymns.

Periodically, a glass jar of dried peyote is passed around the tepee, chased by several swallows of the bitter peyote tea.

Few foods on Earth taste as bad as peyote, which can easily turn the stomach.

In the center of the tepee is a small fire, carefully tended by the Fire Man, an integral player in the peyote ceremony.

With amazing artistry, he sculpts 10 hours of embers and ash into the glowing image of an eagle in flight.

In the early morning hours, the image appears to rise from the swept red dirt floor as Jackson blows a whistle made from the bone of an eagle's wing.

Embracing the top half of the fire is

an altar—a carefully crafted, three-inch-high sand sculpture in the shape of a long crescent.

Chief Peyote—the bulbous cactus flower—sits atop the crescent of sand, glowing in the heat of the night.

Members of the congregation toss cedar needles onto the fire, which dance and sizzle across the tiny aromatic explosions—a prelude to special prayers and confessions offered during the night.

Speaking a mixture of Navajo and English, Tom humbly confess fears and insecurities about the coming move to Albuquerque.

Tears roll down his check and well up in the eyes of friends and family as they respond with encouragement and stream of consciousness prayers of support.

Tom's wife and three young children are there throughout the night.

Even the children, who slept on colorful Navajo rugs through most of the ceremony, take small amounts of peyote.

As an official organization, the Native American Church dates back to 1918, when it was founded in Oklahoma to fight off an anti-peyote campaign by government officials and Christian missionaries.

It reports a membership of 250,000 American Indians from a variety of tribes.

---

Before going to the school to bring the Bible story, we stopped at the little traditional trading post to deliver the U.S. mail. A small group of Navajo soon gathered around the trader to see what the missionary had brought. Some were looking for their monthly relief checks and others were hoping for a letter from their child in a far away government school.

It was time to go to the little stone school to teach the children. It was a thrill to see the sea of little brown faces with their sparkling brown eyes. How they enjoyed singing the children's choruses, some in English and others in Navajo. They loved to go through the songs with motions. A person couldn't help but fall in love with these little children of the desert. How we thanked God for the opportunity to teach them of Jesus and his love and we longed that they might turn to the living God.

Some parents had also joined their children to hear what the missionaries had to say. We didn't know if they were curious, interested, or just waiting for a ride as we returned to Shiprock. Whatever the reason, they were receiving the precious truth of God's Word. It is encouraging to know that God's Word does not return to Him void.

After the Bible lesson was told, the parents said a few words to the children, handed them some candy and gum they had gotten from the trading post, and then gave their little ones a tender embrace and left. Our hearts went out to them as we saw the little kids fight hard to keep the tears back. How they would like to go home, even if it meant sleeping on the hard adobe ground on sheep skins. The kids walked out to follow the horses and wagons to see their little sister perched proudly on a sack of flour with her pet lamb in her arms. They watched until the team had crossed the knee deep San Juan river and climbed out over the hill and disappeared. We felt like putting our arms around the little tykes to cheer them up but felt we didn't know them long enough to get their confidence. We longed to have them know the Good Shepherd well enough to get comfort by going to Him. We would pray for them and many others in Government boarding schools on and off the reservation. Often they went thousands of miles away to other states. Parents nor children could write well so, they seldom heard from each other.

Before starting our long trip home we decided to get a bottle of pop at the trading post and try to befriend the Indians there. It wasn't easy because any small talk would have to be done through an interpreter. Some looked our way and nodded, but we couldn't tell if they were friendly or indifferent. Other missionaries had said it would take time to get acquainted. A young couple came over to where we were standing and asked if they could ride home with us. The young mother had a darling little baby on a cradle board and we couldn't help admiring the mother's beautiful shiny velvet blouse decorated with rows of hand made silver shells. Sometimes shiny silver dimes served as buttons from the neckline down to the waist. A most beautiful belt made of large silver buckles and crowned with blue turquoise was worn by both the young people. The young lady wore an attractive pleated satin skirt which came down below her ankles. A multi-colored wool Pendleton blanket was draped over her arm.

When we were ready to start out, the father got into the cab and the young mother and infant sat in the rear. I felt sorry for the lady and child as we were jostled by the rutty roads and as the air became crispy cold. Later, we found out that it was generally the custom for the men to sit in the cabs of the pickups while the women and children rode in the back. This custom gradually changed as time went on.
It was a great feeling to arrive home in Shiprock safely and sit down to a good warm meal with the little family. We closed our meal with thanksgiving to God for the opportunity to sow the Word again. As we tucked the children in bed, we asked God to take care of our Navajo friends and help them understand the Gospel message and receive Christ as their Savior.

We never know what will impress our little children as they hear us talk of our experiences and hear us pray earnestly for others to be saved. Sally Ann was four years old at this time. One day, while playing out by the back porch with little Navajo children of the Begay family, we heard her telling them about Jesus and how they must believe in Him to be able to go to heaven. When they said they would, she came hurriedly into the house and said "Daddy, will you baptize my friends? They believe in Jesus!" How this thrilled our hearts.

Now some thirty-five years later the children are grown and we know of some who are serving the Lord in

Shiprock. They like to remind us of how we gave them cookies when they came to play or visit. A kind word or loving deed in Jesus' name will bear fruit. It is not always visible or known at the time. Jesus did promise that if we gave a cup of water to the least of these little ones, we would not lose our reward.

A recent article in the "Christian Indian" told of one of those children, Rose Johnson, now an adult, who went with others to an Indian tribe way up in Canada to bring the Gospel. She and her husband sing beautiful duets. We sowed some seeds, others watered and God gives the increase! To Him be the glory.

**Navajo mother with her children.**

Teec Nos Pos Mission – 1953, Chapel with study room on right, Kruis home in middle, and interpreters home on right.

## Chapter IV

# LIFE AT TEEC NOS POS

After assisting Rev. Vander Stoep in Shiprock for a year and a half, we were asked by Rev. Evenhouse, the new secretary of the Foreign Mission Board, to take up the work at Teec Nos Pos, an isolated post having only a small trading post, traders' residences, a three grade school and teacherage, our home, chapel, and interpreter's home. We had gotten a little acquainted with that field by going there to conduct Sunday afternoon services and visiting some of the camps during the trip from Shiprock. One or more Indian homes was termed a "camp."

The trip from Shiprock was a long , rocky thirty miles. At the time several of the arroyos had no bridges and often were flowing with rushing muddy water created by sudden, late summer flash floods. Because of the winding, rough, roads it took about an hour to go one way.

We had to make this trip at least once a month to do our shopping in Farmington which was sixty miles east. This was an all day affair with our little children, which had its humorous sidelines as well as being tiresome. It could even be dangerous when the adobe roads became gooey. Mae had the biggest burden of these trips getting the family ready for their personal needs. I just thank the Lord for her strengths and many willing adjustments to the frontier life. It was like pioneering because of the hardships in a different cultural setting. Very few of the Indians had cars or trucks at that time and often would ask us to take them along to town or to the hospital. Our hearts said "yes" but usually space wouldn't permit a "yes".

At times, the Navajo would come with a sick child or a pregnant mother almost ready to deliver, to request a ride to Shiprock. We felt very distressed, and yet compassionate when we saw that the sick patient had perhaps waited too long to be helped, because they had to first be treated by a medicine man at a sing or squaw dance.

One time, a call came from the teacher at Beclabito School, which was 10 miles east. She asked us to hurry and come because Helen Begay, who lived near the school, had a new baby who was very ill. She asked if we could take them to the Shiprock Hospital. We hurried over the rough road as fast as we dared to go. Mae took her thermometer along and found that the baby had a temperature of 106 degrees or more. Mae tried to bring the temperature down by giving him a cool sponge bath. Then we decided to rush him to Shiprock. The child was turning blue. Mae decided he wasn't able to get enough oxygen, so she held him upside down and gave artificial respiration which helped him expel the mucous. It was a tense 20 rough miles filled with fervent prayers to the Great Physician, Healer of body and souls.

When the Doctor at the Public Health hospital examined the baby, the temperature was still way up there. God answered our prayer and used the Doctor's skills and medications to save the baby's life. We were so thankful that the high fever didn't cause brain damage. Mae has been calling that baby her son and no wonder! He is now a grown man. His mother is still serving the Lord, but her husband has never accepted Christ as his Savior and Lord. It has been a hard life for Helen.

The Teec Nos Pos Mission was formerly called Carisso Mission because it was located at the base of the beautiful Carisso Mountains. The name Teec Nos Pos describes a huge round cottonwood tree which stood for years out in a field. When we were at Teec Nos Pos, the little children crowded into the small chapel each Sunday morning for Bible stories and songs, which they sang lustily in Navajo and English. The songs which they chose most often were the action choruses and "There'll be no Dark Valley", "Come Thou Fount", and "Jesus Loves Me". They also came to the chapel once during the week after school. I was thankful Mae could come from next door to play the piano for our meetings.

We had Sunday morning services in the stone school house at Beclabito. We would take the little portable organ along. When the teachers, Mr. and Mrs. Henderson, and the caretaker were gone, we held the service outside under the Chinese elm trees. I think the children liked that because they didn't have to sit so quietly and they enjoyed watching or playing with the dogs and goats that came around. The Indian children often had a pet lamb or a little kid (goat) with them.

**School children at Biclabito.**

At first, the attendance at the services was very small. I recall a time when Ed McKenzie (the interpreter) and I made the 32 mile trip and no-one came. Slowly, the Lord added those who were being saved. These Christians became very dear to us. We would speak of them as "shi ma" (my mother) and "shi deezha" (younger sister), etc. as the Navajo did. If we didn't know if they were older or younger, we could just say "shi la'", Shi being a prefix denoting possession.

Mae taught Sally kindergarten at home by correspondence. Later, Sally and Rick went to the boarding school. Mae taught Sally 3rd and 4th grade by correspondence, but when our family grew to six children it got too much for Mae and we put Sally in the Rehoboth Boarding School near Gallup, which was 130 mile away. It was against school policy for the white children to stay in the Indian dorms, so she and others stayed in the white children's house. This was a hardship and often a heart rending experience. It was too far to get the children home every weekend, so we had arrangements with a family at Rehoboth for her to stay there on weekends. When Vander Stoep's children came home, they often took Sally along and we picked her up in Shiprock and brought her back on Monday morning.

We loved our work and our home life at Teec Nos Pos even though there were some hardships. The only electricity we had was from six until nine in the evenings when the government school was running the gasoline operated generator. The voltage dropped considerably in the evening when there was too much use by us and the interpreter. We had to be careful not to use the appliances at the same time. One time, our washing machine motor burned out. My interpreter didn't understand what burned out meant, so he didn't let us know when they were washing.

We had given them the choice of time. Often, we expected the Indians to understand our cultural language. When we told the interpreter what happened, he said, "Why don't you talk straight?"

Because we didn't have electricity during the day, we built our own cooler using a slotted box covered with burlap and put in a window and then kept wet by running water over it. This kept the box somewhat cool so we could put perishables in it. Of course it wasn't as efficient as a refrigerator. We couldn't keep meat very long so we often bought mutton at the local trading post. It wasn't long before we enjoyed it and to this day, we try to have mutton stew, roast, steak, and ribs when the kids come home. One of my favorite slides is one of our family sitting around the table on Christmas Eve chewing on ribs. It was a delicious Christmas Eve dinner. The children looked so happy and healthy with faces shining with mutton grease, and eating delicious fried bread. After the children were put to bed, we had a little time to think back about previous Christmas eves in our childhood. On those occasions we felt lonesome for relatives and friends.

**_Kruis family at 1955 Christmas dinner._**

We never went home for the holidays because those were important times to celebrate in the churches and schools. We also were invited to go to homes and chapter houses to bring Christmas messages. I recall with pleasure the evening we went to the Benally home at Teec Nos Pos. I don't think any of the family were Christians, but they had heard the Word at various times. How we longed and prayed that the family would accept the Christ of Bethlehem as their Savior and Lord. Three of the young girls became Christians and today are serving the Lord faithfully. One of the girls, Lilly, later served with us as our interpreter's wife and led a ladies' Bible study at another church when they moved to another area.

Christmas was always a busy time. Besides having our church festivities we handed out small gifts and little sacks including candy, an orange and peanuts to the many children in the boarding schools. We missionaries from Teec Nos Pos, Red Rock and Shiprock got together at Shiprock to sack the goodies in an assembly line fashion.

Mae and I went to the countryside just before Christmas to distribute bags of groceries to poor families. This was a joyous experience. Some times members of the churches

**Hauling water at Red Mesa**

*That They Might Know*

would go along to help us sing Christmas Carols in Navajo and English. We also got together to assemble calendars printed up by the Navajo Gospel Time Radio Committee. It was such a blessing to receive gifts sent by supporting friends around the country to help us with this commemoration of God's unspeakable gift of love. The Creston Christian Reformed Church people of Grand Rapids did a lot for us on these occasions.

Our children enjoyed the free, open life in the beautiful canyon where our chapel and home were located. Our favorite pastimes were family picnics and hiking. Some times Sally, Rick and I went hunting for cottontails up the mesa across from the mission. One time, we were successful, bringing home three bunnies using a single shot .22 rifle. Before we got back, we were very thirsty. Sally was about seven years old at the time. She said, "Dad, when Moses was in the desert he made water come out of the rock. Can't you do that for us too?" I had to think fast. I didn't want her to lose her childlike faith in God. I told her, "We can make it back to the house alright. Sometimes it is good for us to suffer some hardship so we can understand other's suffering better and be more ready to help them." This seemed to satisfy her.

The children would watch with awe as the Indians came to get water from a faucet in the yard. The water was sweet and cold. It seeped from the hill in back of the house and was collected in a concrete tank on the hillside. So we had good running water

**Trudy & Dan Kruis**

which we appreciated very much. The children liked to catch rides on the rumbling wagons as they came up from the trading post. At times we played Gospel songs and messages on hand wound machines near the faucet, trying by all means to win some.

There wasn't much opportunity for swimming but the children took advantage of some fast flowing muddy water in the wash across from our house after a flash flood. The white children looked about as brown as the Indians.

Sally picked up the Navajo language quite readily as she played and went to school with the Navajo children. We were told that she had really good diction, which isn't easy for us Anglos. Later in life, she was able to work in Albuquerque helping to develop bilingual reading materials. Rick spent a lot of time outside by himself, enjoying the animals and birds. Later, Danny was a close companion. When Rick was around two years old, he would say, "Those are my horses," whenever he saw horses along the road. He had a lot of them.

One day when my interpreter and I were out calling, we met some men picking up old horses and donkeys to haul to processing plants for dog or cat food (I trust). As they were about to load up a baby burro, I asked how much he would take for him. I bought it for $5.00 and took it home in the pickup. The little fellow, who we named Bahe, which means grey, soon became a close member of the family, even following the children into the house. Of course he didn't stay long. Sometimes Trudy and Dan would use him for a pillow out in the yard when he was lying in the warm sunshine. When he was nearly full grown, he got pretty spunky and bucked Rick off. He broke his arm and we had to take him 130 miles to have a cast put on. Later, we sold the donkey for ten dollars to our interpreter's

*That They Might Know*

father, Frank Talley, at Tohlakai. Bahe helped Frank herd sheep for many years. The children saw Bahe often, because a few years later, we did mission work in the Tohlakai area.

One of our concerns was that rattlesnakes might strike one of the family. One day as Rick was going down to feed the chickens across the road, he came about a foot away from a coiled rattler. He didn't seem to realize the danger because he came back as cool as a cucumber and told me what he had seen. I grabbed a long handled shovel and went down to where it was coiled under the corner of an old wagon box, and soon the rattler was headless.

Another time, when Mae was cleaning the chapel, she went out to empty the dustpan and there was a rattler coiled by the steps. This one didn't rattle, because he must have been asleep. She tried to get help from the school, but the Navajo were afraid to kill them. She threw stones at it, but it got away. We were thankful that they usually rattled before striking, but they still give one the shivers. One time, as Mae went down the steps into the partial basement, she saw a huge bull snake at the bottom and let out a scream. Bull snakes are good friends keeping rodents and rattlers away, but we didn't care for them in the basement. When the boys grew older, they enjoyed handling them.

Once I skinned a large rattler for the skin. I brought the skinned snake in the house to show how good it looked. An elderly Navajo woman happened to be in the kitchen and let out a scream. Needless to say, we didn't eat the thing.

Later one morning, this old grandma came back quite early in the morning. We couldn't understand her sign language. Mae thought she might be hungry so fixed her a cheese sandwich after we finished breakfast. The children looked in awe at the old wrinkled face partly hidden by her disheveled white hair. I suppose they thought she must be almost two hundred years old. She was known as "Saani Apple" (Old Lady Apple), because she lived in a small unkempt apple orchard. Refusing the cheese sandwich, she got up off the floor where she sat cross-legged and held her hands to her nose. We decided to send for Jimmy, our interpreter, from next door. She made a most unusual request. In the past, we had gotten many requests for help but this topped them all.

Mrs. Apple's horse had died and the body was lying on the edge of an arroyo near her house. It was decaying in the hot sun, drawing hundreds of flies and hungry dogs, and smelling bad. We were asked if we could help her get rid of the carcass. While we liked to help people in trouble, this just didn't seem to be in line with our calling. Jimmy said she didn't have relatives nearby, so perhaps we could drop by her place on our way to visit homes in her area and throw some kerosene or gasoline over the critter and add a couple of old car tires and set fire to it. By doing this we might prevent the spread of possible diseases. So we did, but at least we didn't have to conduct a funeral.

The saddest part of our work were the many burials we were asked to help with. I recall one young couple coming with their horse and wagon. We could see they were mourning. They led us to the wagon and uncovered a deceased infant. They pleaded with us to prepare the baby for burial. Mae washed and dressed the baby, but the parents were afraid to even look at their precious child for the last time. Mae couldn't keep the tears back. Our hearts went out to them and we hoped this experience would lead them to put their trust in the Lord of life. We carried the remains to a little burial plot some distance away across from the mission.

There were times of anxiety being so far from our doctor at Rehoboth (130 miles away). One Sunday morning, I opened the porch window to call to my interpreter about something, when suddenly the window fell down. Trudy Lynn, who was about three and a half years old, had her hand on the window sill without my knowledge. Her middle finger got caught, nearly severing the tip. I asked Jimmy to take care of the Sunday School and morning service as best he could. We were so thankful that Mae's sister, Helen, was visiting from Everett, Washington, and could stay to care for the other children and help Jimmy. She played the piano for the services. We decided we should go as fast as we could safely to Farmington 60 miles to the east to have the end of the finger sewed back on. When I saw the threaded needle penetrate the flesh, I began to faint and had to leave the room. Again, I thanked the Lord for Mae's nursing experience and courage. Later, the finger had to be treated for infection but thanks to the Lord's goodness and healing mercies it became well.

**Trudy Lynn**

On another occasion, when Mae was having labor pains, we decided we should leave for Rehoboth. Hilda Friedsma, the Bible Woman at Shiprock, had told us we could leave the four children with her if she were at home when such an occasion arose. It was about eleven o'clock at night when we rudely awakened her with four sleepy-eyed children at her door. She didn't wait for our apology, but cheerfully invited us all in. We couldn't wait to help put the kids to bed. I had been visiting homes all day and was very tired. When we got near Tohatchi, 30 miles from Rehoboth, I became too sleepy to drive on. I had to lay my head on the steering wheel and nap a while. Pretty soon, Mae shook me awake saying, "We better get going, the pains are about five minutes apart." I replied, "Five minutes apart?! I guess so." I recalled stories of missionaries having to deliver babies in the cab of a pickup. That wasn't for me, nor Mae, I'm sure. When we got to Gallup, a long freight train crossed in front of us on the Santa Fe tracks. The upshot of it was that Robert James (Bob) wasn't born until about 6 AM. We rejoiced again in God's good favor, giving us another bouncing boy.

I was sorry I couldn't stay with Mae and the baby a while, but had to hurry back to pick up the children in Shiprock. Of course, the first thing I heard were loud shouts, "What is it, Dad?" I can't recall what gender was wanted, but we had two boys and two girls, so none could complain. Of course, there were a lot of questions like, "When is Mom coming home?" "What's his name?" "When was he born?" "Is he cute?" and "I get to hold him first."

When we knew we were going to have another child (Ed), I decided Mae had more than enough work and shouldn't try teaching Sally and Rick at home. The secretary of the Mission Board agreed and told us there was a vacancy 12 miles north of Gallup at Tohlakai. We accepted that appointment but were reluctant to leave the friends at Teec Nos Pos and Beclabito. When we were all packed and ready to leave, we had one of those famous flash floods sending torrents of muddy water rushing down the rocky or clay arroyos. We had to wait for the water to subside so we could cross the arroyo and go on our way. The children understandably would get pretty restless in their crowded positions but enjoyed watching the madly rushing water as it carried interesting objects of debris bobbing up and down. We got to Rehoboth around midnight that night as it rained all the way. The people there had been worried about us.

*That They Might Know*

**Hauling water at Red Mesa**

## Chapter V

# CAMP WORK EXPERIENCES

**W**e call visiting homes out in the country 'Camp Work' because the houses or hogans are in small groups or camps. Perhaps they were called camps because, in the older days, the dwellings in summer were often outside shelters made of branches lain over poles. The Navajo word for this shelter is "Cha ha' oh", or shade. A hat is a "Cha ha'", or shade. The dwellings could also be tents especially during lambing time in the spring.

I recall visiting in one tent in which they had a stove. The sparks from the stove must have landed on the canvas because there were many small holes in it. This stands out in my memory because it was here that LuLu Nez committed her life to Christ. It was such a thrill, I couldn't hold back my tears of joy and neither could my interpreter. This was the first visible fruit of our work among the Navajo Indians. She was such a faithful and loving child of God. Some thirty years later, this dear saint was killed in a highway accident and the family remembered that we had led her to the Lord, so they asked me to come to Shiprock to conduct her funeral. Many family members and friends, whom I hadn't seen for many years, were there. It was a reunion of sadness and joy. Young people came up and said "Do you remember me?"

Now, going back to other early campwork experiences, I can say that although we visited many homes in the Shiprock area where we first lived and worked under Rev.

F. Vander Stoep, I recall more of the visits out in the more remote areas of the reservation. One day, Sampson Yazzie and I had to go out to Red Rock, now called Red Valley, to teach Bible in the elementary school on released time. Sampson was quite upset because this trip came up unexpectedly. We had to go about 25 miles, so decided to visit some homes on the way. Samson didn't say a word all the way. I tried to open a conversation and used some humor. Later, I learned that was the wrong approach. It's better to be still for a while.

When we came to the stone hogan of Harriet Cadman, I didn't know what to do. Harriet understood and spoke very little English. I understood and knew very little Navajo. I could greet her with the usual "Ya at' eh'" (good). Samson left without saying a word and hiked over a nearby hill. I felt very uncomfortable. After greeting Harriet, I gave her a few Sunday school papers, hoping her children would read them to her. As I was ready to leave, Samson reappeared. We went back in the home and had a pleasant visit. During our lunch time, Samson and I had a good talk. I learned more about the Navajo culture but had a lot more to learn about how to relate to our Navajo people and their ways. We should have had some in depth orientation before beginning our work.

[After about 35 years it was such a pleasure to meet Harriet in the church at Red Valley and to know that she is still serving the Lord faithfully.]

During the early years of our work, most of the hogans were made of piñon logs notched at the ends to fit so that the logs needed little chinking with tree bark or adobe clay. The roof was made by crisscrossing layers of small tree trunks or limbs so that they formed a dome. At the peak of this dome, a square hole was left for ventilation. Often a fifty-five gallon oil drum was used for a stove. The drum was open on the bottom with a piece cut where the fire was built for heat and to cook over. Often there was a mouth watering aroma filling the room, coming from roasting mutton ribs or baking tortillas on a grill made of twisted bailing wire. I admired the ingenious inventions of our friends. A stove pipe was fitted into a hole in the top of the barrel, and extended up through the hole in the roof.

Sometimes the homes were made of sandstone formed by skillful stone masons. The Navajo have many manual skills. I have been surprised how quickly the sheep herders caught on to the mechanical workings of the "chidi'" (car). However, many cars ended up dead in the yard. But, most of the time in early days, the "shade tree mechanic" could only afford a run down car or pickup.

The sandstone and log hogans usually had packed adobe floors and on hot days would be sprinkled to cool the home. This was a cooling system that worked quite well and cost nothing.

Many homes had no windows but got their light from a large opening in the center of the roof and in summer, the open door. Flies had easy access and frequently a cat would be warming itself at the hole and watching events below.

The doors of the home were usually homemade and always faced east. This was convenient for those who prayed looking toward the sunrise to begin their day. This religious practice was also a blessing in the providence of God for this door facing east caused the home to be protected from the strong westerly wind's cold blast as well as the spring dust storms.

The Navajo are a very hospitable people and usually offer something to sit on which could be a small bench or a rolled up mattress. They often offer a cup of coffee which has been brewing for some time on the old oil drum or hot coals on the earthen floor.

In the olden days, we missionaries always carried a small box of medications such as toothache drops, liniment, pink corrective mixture for diarrhea, and small cans of ointment to treat impetigo. Impetigo are ugly festering scabby sores often covering much of the face and arms of small children and babies. It is hard for children to quit scratching the sorry looking skin. The sores were treated by scrubbing with soap and water and covering them with sulfa ointment.

Today the children are given Penicillin shots, which clear it up much more quickly. The missionaries no longer carry medications since the people have more ready access to the clinics. Also, the homes are more sanitary and most of them have running water or more convenient access to a water supply. Formerly, water had to be hauled quite long distances in old oil drums which were covered with cloth from flour sacks to eliminate splashing over on the rutty and stony trails. I marvel that half or more of the water didn't splash out.

Many little children died of dehydration due to extreme diarrhea. It was so painful for parents and us to see the cute little ones waste away before they could get help. Often they tried the medicine man's ceremony before getting the child to the clinic or hospital. Parents found it so hard to refuse little ones the new melons, fall corn, and other fruits. We often saw a small child chewing on a green melon rind which had been covered with flies.

*That They Might Know*

In most areas, wood had to be hauled long distances by wagon or pickups. The wood (cedar or pinon) was found on higher elevations on high mesas or mountain tops. It troubled me to see this scarce wood burn so furiously in their drum stoves or often, flat top, small laundry stoves. I tried to encourage the people to use dampers in their stove pipes to regulate the draft. I saw dampers at the trading posts. Maybe something in their culture made it unacceptable to use the damper. It troubled me to see large flames shooting out of the stove pipes above the roof top when wood hauling was such a task.

The hogans were usually very comfortable and the odor of burning cedar in open fires made it more homey. I enjoyed watching large white snowflakes floating down through the hole in the dome into the home and hearing the sizzling of snow when it hit the hot stove.

During earlier years of our campwork, we found more people at home and more ready to listen because they had few cars and trucks to leave with and no television to interfere. Because the people lived in such isolation, they were glad to see someone to talk to. There were no phones out there so when a person became sick, someone had to go on horseback or wagon to the trading post or mission to get help. There were many anxious hours for the women who were left alone because the husbands were working in some far away place on the railroad. Our campwork was often interrupted when seriously ill persons or mothers in labor asked to be taken to the hospital. The trips were usually 30 or 40 miles. These were difficult decisions to make because it deprived us of precious time to bring the gospel, but showing mercy was also important to our work.

On one occasion, a woman was brought to the mission having labor pains. Mae's sister was visiting at the time, so Mae and I took Mrs. Begay to Shiprock. It was late at night when we started back. We were both worn out and became so sleepy we couldn't go on. We stopped on the roadside and slept a while on a mattress in the back of the pickup. The next day Mrs. Begay came back to the mission! It had been false labor. From then on, Mae decided to examine a person before taking her in. Mae's nursing experience as an R.N. was a blessing for our family and the Navajo in those isolated areas.

Another time, when it was already dark, a man by the name of Salt Clah came on horse back from Red Mesa, a distance of about 14 miles. Mr. Clah asked if we would please come to his hogan, because his wife was ready to have a baby. Mae and Jimmy, our interpreter, went out there with the mission truck while I stayed with our children. There was a bitter cold wind blowing, but it was nice and warm inside. Mrs. Clah offered Mae and Jimmy a cup of hot coffee. Mae was prepared. She had thought of taking a sheet and scissors along. The mother wasn't ready to deliver but later we heard that all went well with her.

Little children had to accept a lot of responsibility early in life because they were often left alone while the mother was out herding sheep. Little kids under school age carried wood in, built fires and even fed younger ones. We would come in and try to cheer them up, but usually they just looked with those deep brown eyes in a mystified way.

When the mothers were home they could spend a lot of time with the little ones because in the one room, dirt floor hogan there wasn't much housework, and meals were pretty simple but good, especially fried bread. In the early days, there was usually a steel cot or bed and the rest of the

*That They Might Know*

family slept on the ground on sheep skins or mattresses which were rolled up and lay against the sides in the daytime. There was usually a small table and homemade cupboard. There would be a bucket of water with a dipper hanging on it from which all could drink. There was no refrigeration so the water was usually quite warm. It's no wonder they couldn't resist the cold pop at the trading post when they went there. The trading posts were usually well stocked. The Navajo often bought cases of pop. Consequently, most children had bad teeth.

The trading posts were usually operated by Mormon Anglos. I always felt sorry for the Navajo because they traded their lambs, wool, and rugs for groceries which were a much higher price than we had to pay in town. They could buy groceries and household needs on credit with promise to pay when they brought in their rugs, wool, sheep or cattle. They often pawned their rifles, jewelry, saddles or other belongings when they had an emergency or needed something for which they didn't have cash. Because of this, the people were obligated to the trader to trade at his post. Traders usually took care of the U.S. mail so they were able to hold the government checks. The trader often did come to the aid of the Indians in their needs too. I know it wasn't easy for the traders to know how long he could carry a person on credit. I suppose there were often losses. Consequently, the prices had to be high.

Related to campwork were our funeral services. The Navajo were fearful of death and needed comforting help when loved ones passed away. In former days, the people seldom had lumber around from which to make caskets. We often helped them out. At one mission post, there was a pile of lumber for just such emergencies. At times, the deceased would be a long way from the mission. When someone came for help we had to ask for the size of the departed one. On one occasion we took lumber along and had to carry it quite far, because there wasn't a road or trail for the pickup all the way. The family offered us a sheep if we (my interpreter and I) would wash the body and dress him with new clothes they had. We took care of that, but then found out the body was too long for the coffin. What should we do now? In the first place, we couldn't bend his arms to get them in the coat sleeves. We were glad the relatives weren't around then, because we had to slit the suit coat down the back and then bend the legs at the knees. We put his shoes along side of the body. He wouldn't be wearing them anyway. I assure you, this wasn't a comfortable situation, for us at least. Jimmy was glad to get the sheep.

While I was still working from Shiprock, Samson and I were on our way to Redrock when a Navajo man waved us down. He made a strange request. The highway department was grading the road there when they struck a wood coffin, the corner of which was protruding about a foot out of the embankment. The man who hailed us down explained that his brother had been buried there about 14 years earlier and asked us if we would be willing to move the coffin some place else. We could understand his feelings about the matter. After talking it over, we decided we shouldn't get involved, but we would ask the government agent in Shiprock, who was supervisor of that area under the Bureau of Indian Affairs, if he would take care of the problem. I don't know if he did or not. We were concerned that the coffin might fall to pieces, and then what? Besides, we might be feared or under suspicion by some who knew we had this contact with the dead. That night, I had a scary dream in which I had gone down into the basement of a mortuary and saw a row of caskets all open, and in one of them my older brother was sitting up. I broke out in a cold

*That They Might Know*

sweat. I mention this because I don't want to leave the impression that we Anglos don't have uncomfortable and even scary feelings about death at times.

Another sad occasion was the burial of a little 4 year old boy. It was midwinter, and the little boy had gone with his mother to the river to fetch some water. He slid on the ice bordering the river into the ice cold water and drowned. His mother tried in vain to rescue him from the fast flowing stream.

The father came by team and wagon to the mission to get help. We made arrangements to go the five or six miles over rugged terrain to the bank of the river to meet the man. We climbed into his rickety wagon which looked as if it would fall apart any minute, and down the bank we went. There was three or four feet of ice along the fast flowing river. The poor horses slid down the ice into the water. As the wagon rumbled, shook, and jarred its way over the immersed rocks and boulders, we held our breath for fear the rickety wagon would fall apart. In midstream, the water reached within a few inches of the wagon box floor. I didn't look forward to the return trip, but with the Lord's good care, we made it without a cold bath.

When we arrived on the hill and came to the hogan, we were met by a family member who offered us an old worn pick. Jimmy and I and one of the men hacked away at the dry frozen ground. It was a bitterly cold, windy day. Jimmy and I decided to take some wood off an old dilapidated hogan nearby with which to build a fire to keep warm by turns. To my sorrow, I was to learn later that the hogan was a "che'indee" or spirit hogan, and it was forbidden to enter one or remove anything from it. Very likely, someone had died in it.

We couldn't get the grave dug very deep. We had a short committal service, trying to give a meaningful, comforting message. This is always difficult when the bereaved don't know the Great Comforter of souls.

It was years later that we finally conducted a funeral for a believer. It troubled me that burials became a routine affair without real feeling. I prayed about it. Later, we were to know in a very personal way.

While we are on the subject of burials, I want to relate another incident. Old Mr. Ute, father of friends who came to our services, passed away. We were asked to help with the burial. The grave had been dug a short distance from the family camp. The family had built the box and prepared the body. Usually, the family encloses personal belongings such as jewelry, shawl, hat and even money. After the lid had been nailed shut, a son realized he had not enclosed two silver and turquoise rings. The family members wouldn't want to wear the rings, so after a little discussion decided to give them to me, saying I wouldn't be afraid to wear them. I gave one to John Tally, my interpreter at the time.

I am reminded of another incident that happened when we were still in Shiprock. We were visiting the saltwater home near Teec Nos Pos. The mother came out to us crying. Her grown son was very ill. In fact, he was so thin, he could hardly walk. Mrs. Saltwater pleaded with us to take her son to the Public Health Hospital in Ft. Defiance. When I got home, I asked Rev. Vander Stoep if I should bring him to the hospital. The next day, I made the long trip with my Chevy van putting a mattress on the floor for the patient to lie on. When I got to the hospital, the doctor examined the man and, in an angry voice said, "You take him back home.

We can't do anything for him. He will die in a day or two. When you get home, I want you to burn that mattress and scrub out your van with hot soapy water. If you want to get TB, just keep hauling people like him around." Needless to say, I followed the Doctor's orders.

A couple of days later, on our way to church, we stopped by the Saltwater home again to see the patient. Two men were just coming over the hill wearing just loin cloths and carrying spades. Their bodies were gray. They had rubbed down with wood ashes. I was told it was done to ward off evil spirits. It was a sad and difficult time for us and the Navajo family.

**Harriet Cadman, an early convert.**

**Sampson Yazzie and Mr. Kruis at
Red Valley in June of 1953**

## Chapter VI

# USING AN INTERPRETER, ADVANTAGES AND DRAWBACKS

*T*here was only one mission post where I didn't have to use an interpreter, sometimes called an interrupter. I often desired that the Lord would give me the gift of tongues, especially the Navajo tongue. I prayed that I could learn the language much more readily. I enjoyed trying to use the little Navajo I had learned, at least thought I knew.

Shortly after I arrived on the field, we stopped at a home where we had visited before and saw a small boy who was sick. I wanted to ask the mother how her son was now. Instead of asking how her son was, I asked "How are your lice?" The Navajo word sounded similar to me. My interpreter, Samson Yazzie, at the time, laughed along with the mother. I asked what was wrong and he explained to me. I found the Navajo people to be very gracious and usually corrected us with a pleasant smile.

The interpreters didn't have an easy task. In fact the success of our work depended a great deal on their abilities and attitudes. Most of the interpreters hadn't been Christians very long and then an awful lot of Biblical terms such as righteousness, redemption, salvation, sanctification, etc., were abstract terms not easy to explain, even for us.

It's no wonder the interpretation was quite a bit longer than the English message. At first I couldn't understand why the interpreter talked so long. They often added their own illustrations, which was fine and often more applicable to their culture, and they would enhance the message.

A problem earlier missionaries experienced was using interpreters who were not Christians. Christians in the audience would later tell that the interpreter would explain, "That's what the missionary says, but I don't believe it myself."

Having to face the opposition of unbelievers and medicine men wasn't an easy task. The success of our work depended a lot on the courage and faithfulness of the interpreter. I marvel that they could speak so fluently. After saying a few sentences and waiting for him to speak, he would ask what it meant, or to please repeat the words again. I tried to use as simple language as possible.

My first full time interpreter was a young congenial man who loved humor as most Navajo do. Jimmy was recommended to me by Rev. Vander Stoep of Shiprock because he had done some interpreting for him. Jimmy came from an area twelve miles northwest of Teec Nos Pos. His relatives weren't Christians, so we visited them with the gospel frequently. Having worked for some time for an Anglo rancher near Cortez, Colorado, Jimmy had learned some of the white man's ways. His wife, Joella, came from a pagan family about two miles north of our mission. She was interested in the Christian faith and spoke English quite well, but her parents spoke only Navajo.

Jimmy loved children and loved to lead the young school children in choruses and hymns. He played a few songs on his guitar. He was also good with young people. We only had young people's activities during the summer months at first because they were all gone to off reservation schools in Oklahoma, Oregon, California, Nevada, and Utah.

Jimmy loved to pull practical (or not so practical) jokes on people. While visiting homes in his folks' area one day, he came up with one of his pranks. We were eating lunch on one of the small mesas not far off. Some sheep herder had built a cairn of flat rocks in the form of what looked like those Old Testament people used on which to offer sacrifices. I think, for the Navajo, it was just something to do to relieve boredom. Jimmy suddenly got an idea. He said, "Rich, I know where there is an old bleached human skull down there in that wash. Let's get it and put it up on a stick on this pile of rocks." The idea didn't appeal to me. I told him that his people wouldn't like it and might be afraid of it, knowing their fear of death. "It's OK," he said, "I'll take the blame." So he did that.

Sometime later, before going out to work, Jimmy came to me with a worried look on his face and said, "Rich, we are in deep trouble. My half brother, who lives out where `we' put that skull on that stick, has spoken to me. He has been hearing bad noises in his head and the handshaker has determined that it was caused by that skull. He will need a ceremony held over him." Jimmy said the tribe may remove us off the reservation for troubling the people, because we don't respect their sacred customs. He also brought up the occasion when he and I had taken some wood from an old dilapidated and vacated hogan in which someone had died. On another occasion we desecrated a grave by removing a rope and shovel which had been used for burial. I hadn't learned of those taboos or I wouldn't have offended the people (dine').

That incident troubled me greatly, so I decided to visit the people in that area. Nothing was said about the incidents. I concluded later that Jimmy was pulling my leg.

Jimmy told me of another time when he saw tourists taking pictures of the huge "Shiprock", so called because of its appearance like a huge ship sailing on a flat plain. He said to them "Don't you know you could be arrested for taking pictures on our reservation?" When he saw how frightened they became, he told them he was just teasing and had a big laugh at their expense.

I wish I had learned more of the Navajo customs and taboos before beginning my work. I learned that if a person wore some part of an animal or bird, he would take on some of the characteristics of that creature. For instance, to wear eagle feathers would give a person some healing powers or swiftness in running. The owl is a symbol of death so there is great fear if it is heard making its calls on their roof. The same is true if owl feathers are seen floating through the air or lying on the ground. Feathers dropped from a live bird are more powerful than those from a dead bird. The Indians' lives are troubled by many evil omens that can cause serious illness if not observing nature's laws. One must usually rid him or herself of the illness by having a "sing" or ceremony done over the sick one by a medicine man. These ceremonies usually last from three to five days and are very costly to the family. The chants and sand paintings are ways used to bring wholeness where harmony has been interrupted.

One day on my way to work, I picked up a young Navajo man coming back from college in California. He asked who I was and why I was visiting his people's homes. He said they had their own religion and we didn't have to come to change their culture. I told him we didn't come to change their culture, but to bring the Good News of Hope and Salvation and a faith to overcome many of their fears. Jesus came to defeat the powers of Satan and bring peace. Being a faithful Christian does influence religious practices and cultures.

I would like to share the story of my interpreter's early life:

## JIMMY BILEEN'S STORY
### (as told to Creston Sunday School by letter)

*I was born about fourteen miles west of Teec Nos Pos in the Red Mesa area, which is near the Four Corners where Utah, Colorado, New Mexico, and Arizona meet. My parents died when I was about one year old. I don't know how my step-parents got me.*

*When I was about 6 or 7 years old, I started herding sheep alone. Before I was awake someone would grab me off my sheepskin and throw a rope at me and say, "Get the horses." When I got back, I had to take the sheep out. A little piece of blue corn bread was my breakfast. When I got back in the evening, I had to water the horses and chop wood. I was so tired I could hardly stay awake to eat. We ate either sheep meat or horse meat, cornbread and mush most of the time. I often gathered wild plants to be used in soup. We dried them for winter, too. My folks were very poor, so, often, I didn't get much to eat.*

*One time while I was herding sheep an old billy goat got mad at me and started chasing me. I ran as fast as I could, but he caught me just as I got near my hogan. He caught my head between his long horns. I couldn't get loose and he couldn't get rid of me. He dragged me around a long time until he came to the corral. My sister heard me crying and came to set me free. I was bruised all over and* bloody. In a few days, I was back herding sheep. My best friend was my dog, Fuzzy Face.

For clothes, we cut holes in the bottom of burlap sacks and pulled them over our heads. I hardly ever had a haircut and my head was full of sores. I never wore shoes in the summer so my feet got tough like leather from the hot and stony ground. The tops of my feet would get sores and all cracked open. Sometimes, I wrapped cedar bark around my feet to keep them warm, and sometimes, I wrapped some tanned horse hide around them.

One day, I saw other boys and girls in big trucks going to school so I got by the road and when the truck stopped, I got on too. My people didn't know I was running away. I had woman's white high heeled shoes on, a burlap sack for a coat and long dirty hair. I surely got teased when I got in Shiprock. This got me into many fights. I soon got lonesome for home again.

When I was through the fourth grade (12 years old), my half brother took me along to the bean fields in Colorado. I couldn't do much, but the farmer used me to interpret for him. The white man wanted to keep me to do chores, and other errands. I stayed on that ranch in Colorado for eleven years, so I became quite cultured in the Anglo ways, lost most of my Navajo superstitions, and learned the English language quite well.

Later, I came back to the reservation and worked with Rev. Vander Stoep around Shiprock and also helped David Boyd at Teec Nos Pos. After that, I and my new bride, Joella, went to Toadlena to work with Sidney Nez and Rev. Jacob Kobes. Finally I went to work with Geronimo Martin at Teec Nos Pos and then with Rich Kruis.

The End

Jimmy and Joella lived in the interpreter's house next to ours, so I had a good opportunity to instruct Joella regularly in the faith. After a time, she confessed Christ as her Savior and I gave her catechism instruction in preparation for baptism. She was examined in Shiprock with some others, but to our sorrow, she never had the opportunity to make public profession in church and receive baptism.

Jimmy had decided to quit as my interpreter because he had a nervous stomach and frequent pains. He also was losing weight. They went to live in Joella's parents' camp. Jimmy thought the stress of the work was causing his stomach problems.

One Sunday morning as we were coming back from bringing people home from church, I saw a lot of vehicles and wagons parked in the Clah camp. One of the natives told me they were having a ceremony there. This news grieved me greatly. Jimmy and Joella hadn't been coming to church for some time. I just hoped and prayed that they weren't involved and had returned to the native religion. Winning people for the Lord was hard enough without this happening to hinder our witness. Others would probably mock us, as well as a few Christians. These occasions are hard on missionaries at various times. It makes it even harder when traders tell us that the Indians never leave their old religion entirely. "Just wait until one gets sick," they say. Then I must remind myself that the Lord of harvest is still in control. I must remain faithful to Him and be thankful that He was willing to use me at all.

A Bible verse, from Joshua 1, was a comfort to me at times like this. "Have not I commanded thee? Be strong and of a good courage; be not afraid, neither be thou dismayed: for the Lord thy God is with thee whithersoever thou goest." Also I recalled Matthew 28: 19 & 20, especially "Lo,

I am with you always even unto the end of the age." How I needed that comforting word of my Good Shepherd over and over again. At times my faith was pretty weak. It was a comfort to know faithful Christians here and back home were praying. It also helped to come home to a dear wife and children and their activities to relieve the burdened heart, though a heavier burden was soon to come.

It was November of 1956 when we heard that my mother in Wyoming, Michigan, had a serious heart problem and that she might not live very long. We decided we would like to go home to see her. It wasn't easy to make that long trip with our five children and it was hard to leave the Lord's little flock.

The Lord has always been good to us on our long trips to Michigan or to Everett, Washington, where Mae's folks lived. A little book could be written about the humorous events and trials of our many journeys.

When we arrived at the folks home to see mother, we had just gotten in the house when Danny, who was four years old, stood in the middle of the kitchen, looked up with large wistful eyes and said, "Grandma, you are going to die, aren't you?" Grandma Kruis smilingly said "Yes, we are all going to die sometime." Fortunately, Grandma Kruis's health soon showed improvement, so we packed up the kids to make the long journey home again.

**Chapter VII**

# INSTRUCTION IN GOVERNMENT SCHOOLS

*I*n the past, parents of children attending boarding schools had to choose which church they wanted their children to attend for religious instruction. They had to sign up for this. When we first came to the mission field it wasn't difficult for the parents to choose which religious group would instruct their children. Nearly all the missions were either Roman Catholic or Protestant. Our Christian Reformed church was the main protestant church. Most of the children were signed up Christian Reformed, but few of the parents went to the mission churches so didn't really know what was being taught or the difference in their teachings. As far as I know, there wasn't much, if any, recruitment or coercion by missionaries in the homes to get children in their classes. The dorm attendants were glad to have the children gone for those two hours a week and I didn't blame them.

It was difficult to have efficient Bible classes in many of the schools because of the large classes. We were thankful for the opportunity to instruct these children and it was a great joy to see some accept the Lord Jesus as their Savior. The children are so lovable. It was quite picturesque to see all the brown faces, dark brown eyes, and black hair and then the missionaries' and ranchers' children with the contrasting colors of blond hair and pink faces. Children seldom notice the differences. It was an opportunity to get acquainted with parents when we took children home after day school classes, and in the summer have some in Daily Vacation Bible School.

After some years, we were asked by the Mission Board to evaluate the results of this school work. Considering all the time spent in this work, going many miles with mission vehicles and looking at the result, I was negative about it. I felt however, that we couldn't see turning the youngsters over to other groups we felt didn't bring the gospel truths. (By this time the Baptists and Mormons were also conducting classes in several places. We were definitely against sending children to the Mormons.) To this day we are still teaching on released time but the children have a choice whether or not to attend. Consequently, not nearly as many of the children go to classes. I have always been surprised that those who were strong advocates of separation of church and state didn't do more to get these religious classes stopped.

The difficult and often embarrassing time for me was when I had to lead the children in singing. I realized that it was impossible for me to hold a tune without accompaniment which was seldom available. I was so self-conscious when up in front realizing that the older children very likely knew the tune and teachers in the hall might be passing by grinning to themselves. I tried to get the children to start the song with the first word by holding my hands high and bringing them down with the first word, but there was silence. I often asked, "Lord, why couldn't you give me the gift to hear a tune when you called me to this work?"

I recalled what a time my music teacher, Miss Mierop, at RBI had trying to help me. I was so thankful for the times when we were in a school near enough for Mae to come and play the little pump organ or the piano. But then, who

*That They Might Know*

could stay with the little ones at home? I really enjoyed the enthusiastic singing of the kids, especially the action choruses. They chose the same ones nearly every time.

Missionaries from the various posts would often go to a large boarding school some miles away to help in the many classrooms weekly because the enrollment was so large. We went once a week to help the Rev. Vander Stoep and his Bible women, Hilda Friedsma or Hermina Van Dyke. On the way to the various schools, we took our noon lunches with us and did camp work. This was a difficult time for Mae when she was alone with the little children or when the time was near for the delivery of a child. She was very brave and uncomplaining.

While living in Gallup and ministering to the people at Bethlehem Chapel, I was asked to go sixty miles away to Crownpoint to conduct a Bible class to about 250 boarding school children sitting on bleachers in a gymnasium. What a difficult time trying to get and keep the children's attention. Some would be sailing planes. Discipline was made more difficult when we couldn't punish or send them out of the class. There was no one to bring them to a dorm. I often felt the children weren't learning respect for God or His Holy Word, but disrespect. From there, I would have to get in a proper frame of mind to bring God's Word and lead a church family. There was a vacancy at Crownpoint Mission at the time and we missionaries took turns going there.

I went along with workers at Rehoboth weekly, at times, to instruct children in various classrooms at Ft. Wingate. When we could have the same level of children in a classroom situation, the experience was enjoyable and rewarding. I would, when I could, combine two rooms for singing, so another teacher could lead the singing.

**The future looks bright for young child.**

## Chapter VIII

# OUR WORK AT TOHLAKAI

**W**hen we moved to Gallup, my interpreter, John George, with his wife, Mary, and four children stayed on at Teec Nos Pos to carry on the work. Rev. Vander Stoep supervised his work from Shiprock, helping plan his Sunday messages. After a short time the mission board hired Marvin and Ruth Vugteveen to take over the work. We thanked the Lord for bringing this dedicated couple to shepherd His flock there.

We were soon able to hire John and Lillie Tso to work with us in the Bethlehem Chapel area, later called Tohlakai. We knew Lillie as a young high school girl when we were working at Teec Nos Pos. It was an answer to our prayers to have this dedicated, friendly Christian young couple as co-laborers in this needy field.

Tohlakai (white water) was so named because of the grayish white water seeping out of a clay hill. The water was used in that area by the Indians until the shallow well department of the tribe sunk a well for the community. Now many of the homes in the immediate area have clear running water, a luxury for them which we often take for granted. One summer Mae and I borrowed a house trailer from the Rehoboth Mission and moved it to Tohlakai near the old adobe church.

Then we experienced what it was like to haul water and use an outhouse or "hogan yazzie" (little house) as the Navajo call it. We always wanted to live near the people we served to be more available to them. We went back to town to take showers, etc., and it wasn't long before we moved back permanently. John Tso and Lilly lived in a small house trailer near the trading post. They had electricity and water supplied by the trader. John and I did a lot of visiting in the homes in the Rock Springs, Blackhat, China Springs, Twin Lakes and Tohlakai areas. A church in the Chicago area donated a Volkswagen Microbus for our work. This was a great blessing. The people seeing us bouncing up and down the hills over the rough trails would say, "Here come the missionaries in their `loaf of bread', referring to its shape.

John and I tried to get a meeting place in the Black Hat area but that never worked out. One large family, Fred and Lillie Begay, later moved to Tohlakai and became members of the church. Some of the children of the Cheschilly family went to the Rehoboth Mission School and today are helping Rev. Tony Begay with his Campus Fellowship work in Albuquerque.

After a couple of years, John felt led to attend the Reformed Bible Institute in Grand Rapids, Michigan. We knew we would miss John and Lilly very much but were thankful he wanted to improve his usefulness in the Lord's work. When he returned to the Indian Field, the Lord led him to accept the challenge to pastor the church at Church Rock, which nearly bordered the field. So we continued our fellowship with them in the Lord's work. The Lord blessed the ministry greatly under labors of John and Lilly so that the Church Rock church grew in spirit and numbers.

After John Tso left us, John George and family came to Gallup to work with us again for which we were grateful. His family was gifted to lead the singing and provide special music at times. John's wife, Mary, had an elderly mother living in Shiprock. The family went to Shiprock nearly every Saturday to haul water and wood for Mary's mother. I was always concerned that they wouldn't make it back to Tohlakai in time for Sunday services. John and Mary and their four children lived near us in Gallup making it convenient to study and have devotions together.

We held meetings for a while in the twin Lakes Chapter House. As a result of those meetings, the Manuelito family became members of our church at Tohlakai. After we left the work at Tohlakai, we learned about the sad news of Mr. Manuelito's death due to a tragic car accident and since then, Mrs. Manuelito has returned to peyote worship with her relatives. How these people need our prayers and constant pastoral visits! Satan always works to recapture all he can in whatever way he can.

We often visited Ruby Begay living about a mile from the church in the Orlie camp with her two children. Ruby and other members from that camp came regularly to church. Even though Ruby was deaf and couldn't talk, she attended church services, ladies aid and prayer meetings faithfully. Her sister, Edith Watson, was very helpful in interpreting the Bible lessons and the catechism, using sign language. Ruby confessed the Lord as her Savior and was baptized. Another sister, Sarah Long also helped with the sign language. Now after 30 years, Ruby is still faithfully serving the Lord! She puts many to shame who can hear but hear not!

We had an interesting experience one time when John Tso and I were invited by some relatives of the Christians at Bethlehem Chapel to attend special services in their Pentecostal Church. We decided to go because members of our church were asking if the healings they heard about were real. We felt strange in that environment and weren't used to the loud music and shouting. When the leader asked if anyone had a testimony for the Lord, I felt compelled to go up because certainly a missionary of the Gospel should have a message. John Tso then went up and spoke from Matthew 7:21, "Not everyone who says `Lord, Lord', will enter the kingdom of heaven, but only he who does the will of my Father who is in heaven." I think he wanted them to know that being a Christian is more than a lot of emotion but is every day living, pleasing to God.

We heard some strange chattering sounds behind us. The woman was supposed to be speaking in tongues under the power of the Holy Spirit but wasn't edifying anyone because there was no interpretation. The next day John and I went to visit her camp. She was helping with preparation for a ceremony for a member of the family. She felt sheepish because she knew it was inconsistent with her actions the evening before. We had visited that family quite frequently before this, so knew them quite well. This woman had gone to Rehoboth School through the eighth grade and even interpreted for one of our missionaries at times. We are saddened when we know someone had Christian training but didn't respond to it in a positive manner.

Edith Watson, a faithful member of the Bethlehem Church and a Sunday School teacher had a difficult situation at home. She was left with two children as a result of the death of her alcoholic husband. Edith needed a home badly. John Tso and I decided to do something about it. Edith was able to get building materials through the tribal housing authority, so we decided to ask volunteers from Rehoboth to come out and help build the cement block house. There was a good response from carpenters, cement workers, plumbers and electricians and common laborers such as us. It was a real sacrifice for the men to give their

Saturdays off when they could have spent them with their families. That house is still in good use today after 30 years. I am reminded of the Lord's words, "What you have done for the least of these my brethren you have done unto me." Even after some years of living alone in that house, Edith shared it with some of her children who lost their own homes.

On another occasion, a young man of about twenty-two years old who was living with one of the unmarried young women of our church came to our home in Gallup about midnight. The night was clear and bitter cold. Joe was drunk and had been badly beaten. He asked if we could bring him home. We didn't want to bring him to his home in his condition at that time of the night because he wasn't dressed warmly enough to go out in the frigid temperature. We offered to have him sleep on the davenport, but he decided to sleep on the floor in the corner behind the davenport. When we got up in the morning, we discovered that he had left.

Visitors to Gallup often comment about the terrible drinking problem among the Indians. They don't realize that many of the same ones come off the reservation over and over again because liquor isn't allowed on the reservation. However, much is bootlegged. It is a terrible scourge but it isn't only here among Indians.

One Sunday, I was bringing a Father's Day message and telling how important and what a blessing it was to have good fathers, who loved their children. In that way, children would get a good Father-God image. Sitting right in front of me was a darling little Navajo girl looking at me with wonderment as if to say, "What is a father like?" I could hardly go on.

In the summer of 1960, while we were still working at Tohlakai, we bought a large homemade trailer, which was made by two men from the industrial department at Rehoboth, Juke Den Blyker and Ed Berkompas. It was of unusual construction. The upper frame was made of electrical conduit pipe, welded together and covered with hardboard. We could enter the trailer by lifting the frame work up from the rear and placing two support pipes under it to hold it up. It was used for sleeping and baggage. We bought this to take a trip to Washington to visit Mae's parents and sister, Helen and family.

We stopped on our way in Winslow, Arizona, one hundred miles west, to visit former trader friends from Beclabito. While we were in the house, a sudden strong gust of wind came along and blew the top right over onto the heavy tongue, smashing the hardboard. We were thankful the car had been unhitched so it wasn't smashed. What should we do now? We considered going back home and cancel

**Bethlehem Chapel at Tohlakai**

the trip to Mae's parents when Sally heard us and said, "Remember, Mom and Dad, what you taught us? That all things work out for good to those who love the Lord. Can't we trust Him now to take care of this too?" We recalled the Bible verse that says, "A little child shall lead them."

Our friends gave us a large piece of green canvas and some quarter inch rope which we used to cover the frame. We stopped at a hardware store and bought some new canvas and more rope and went on our way again with the nine of us and our "prairie schooner'". What a sight!

Along the way in the desert country on the east border of Nevada, we were stopped by a state patrol officer who told us we had to get side view mirrors that extended further out and better safety chains. We made it to Everett, Washington in good shape! I was ashamed to have that sad looking prairie schooner parked on those neat streets.

We had planned to go on our way to Everett through Zion National Park, but it didn't work out that way. When we arrived near the park, we discovered that some of our children were sick and had very high fevers. It turned out that they were coming down with the mumps. We stayed in a motel that night. We had stopped in Sunnyside, Washington and picked up my brother's 9 year old son, Philip, to go along with us to visit and spend time with our kids. (Philip's mother is Mae's sister and his father is my brother). After we were in Everett a few days, Philip came down with mumps also. His parents thought he had gotten them before. None of the relatives had a large enough house for us all, but they were kind enough to get a large vacant grocery store for us to bunk down in. We were invited out for meals and ate some meals with the whole family at long tables in the store. It was fun.

One night Mae and I came home late and couldn't wake the children to let us in. We knocked and knocked, banged on the windows and after a long time couldn't get anyone to stir. They must have really played that day. We finally found a long cane fishing pole and managed to poke someone through a hole in a window and awakened him. Another difficult event happened on the way home. We were journeying on our way nicely through the semidesert of Idaho, in the heat of the day, when we heard a bumping noise in one of the wheels. It turned out a front wheel bearing had burned out on our Chevy station wagon. A kind state patrol stopped by and offered to call a garage in Burley, Idaho on his short wave radio. A mechanic came out and towed us the 60 miles to Burley and repaired it. Our towing insurance was a real blessing. After that we made it safely home more trials were soon to come.

**Hopeless about the future?**

## Chapter IX

# THE MOVE TO MARYLAND

**W**e had just returned from that adventurous trip to Washington and got back into our work at Tohlakai when Trudy, our 8 year old daughter, became ill. She came in from playing outdoors complaining of aching legs. At first we thought it was "growing pains" but when they didn't get better we decided to take her in for a checkup. Dr. Bos was gone on vacation, so the nurse gave her something for rheumatic fever because she was running a fever. Mae noticed that little red spots, called petechiae, were showing up on her legs. She became suspicious that these were an indication it might be leukemia. She immediately prayed that the Lord would help us to give her up if it was leukemia. She must have had a hard time keeping that idea to herself until Dr. Bos came back. She didn't want me to get upset if it didn't turn out to be leukemia.

When Dr. Bos came back he had blood samples sent to the lab immediately and our worst fears were realized. Our little blond daughter had the dreaded disease, leukemia. Even though Mae had her suspicions, we were both shocked. It was very hard to break the news to our children too. It was hard for them to believe that their sister, who until recently was running and playing outdoors, was going to die.

The support of our family and Christian friends meant so much at that time. We received a lot of comfort and support from our Indian friends at our church at Tohlakai and in other churches in the area. Our neighbors on Zia Drive did all they could to comfort us and offered to help wherever they could. Trudy had a close friend living across the street who was very distressed about the illness. We realized anew what the loving relationship and support of the communion of saints meant and would mean to us in the months ahead. We thank God for the benefit of being in the family of God.

When Trudy first became ill, the indications were that she had rheumatic fever because her blood sedimentation rate was elevated and because of the fever. Later it was discovered that her red blood count was dangerously low and she was hospitalized for blood transfusions. Then we obtained a hospital bed and she came home. Trudy had a beautiful voice and loved to sing hymns and choruses. Sally and Trudy often sang together so I brought my tape recorder and recorded some of their songs. They are precious to us today. We were often reminded of the solo parts Trudy had in the various programs in the little Christian School in Gallup where Miss Lam taught.

Dr. Bos was planning to move away from Rehoboth, so he suggested that we consider taking Trudy to the Public Health Hospital, the National Institutes of Health, in Bethesda, Maryland. He said they just didn't have the facilities to give her proper care in the small Rehoboth Hospital. He also said the research hospital was making some progress in fighting the disease but he didn't give us false hope. Of course, we prayed that a cure would be found, not just for our daughter, but for others who would get the disease.

There were some children that we had heard of who went into remission for a year or two, which gave us some hope. It was a very difficult decision to make. It would mean leaving our mission work and the dear friends at Tohlakai and Rehoboth. How would we manage moving with a family of seven children to a strange city and then to find employment there. After much prayer and deliberation, we decided Mae should go with Trudy and I would stay in Gallup with the rest of the children. Mae and Trudy would return when Trudy went into remission. Then I could continue my work, or rather the Lord's work and the children could continue their schooling at Rehoboth.

It was a sad parting as we embraced one another and said our tearful good-byes in the Albuquerque airport. With five tearful children standing close to the window we waved goodbye as Trudy was wheeled up the ramp into the plane and as Mae and Trudy disappeared into the distance over the Sandia Mountain peaks.

From the airport, we went to the Albuquerque zoo to relieve the children of some of their depressed feelings. The kids were very courageous through it all. Our faith and trust in our heavenly Father's care upheld us and was a great source of strength and comfort. These events took place in the middle of September, 1960

My sister, Ruth Johnson, came after Mae and Trudy left to help with the family, so I could continue with the work at Tohlakai. Later sister, Trena Broersma came to help with the moving and care of the family. Later, others came to Maryland to help out so I could work.

When Mae and Trudy arrived at the NIH hospital in Bethesda, Mae called Rev. Hartwell of the Washington, D.C. Christian Reformed Church, to see if he knew of a place where she could room and board. Dr. and Mrs. Ryskamp, members of the Washington CRC invited Mae (and Trudy, when she was well enough), to stay with them temporarily.

As time went along, it became more difficult for me to be separated from Mae and Trudy. I knew it was difficult for Mae to be away from the other children and me, too. I felt I couldn't do my work efficiently, so we decided we should move to Maryland, too. A real estate sales lady from the church took Mae around to look at houses to buy. We thought it best to buy since rent was terribly high there. Our telephone bills were getting unmanageable, having to call so often about family affairs and housing. We wanted to get settled on something. We decided that I should go to Michigan and leave the six children there with relatives until we could find a house in Maryland.

We were able to sell our house in Gallup to the next door neighbor for the same price we paid for it. It was a good investment for him because he could take over the payments which carried a 4% interest under the V.A. We thought we might have to stay in Maryland a long time, or else we wouldn't have sold it.

After we bought a house near Wheaton Plaza, in Kensington, we went back to Michigan to pick up the family. Trudy was able to go with us. We celebrated Thanksgiving Day with relatives, picked up the children from the various homes and went on our way back to Maryland. We were excited to be united in our own home once more. All the school children except Sally and Rick went to the Washington Christian School. Poor Sally felt so lost and alone at first in the huge Junior High School. Rick was in a smaller grade school.

The first job I got was clerking in a hardware store which only paid $60.00 a week. Then I took over a quick order food counter in a drugstore. That didn't work out profitably. I answered an ad to sell Encyclopedia Brittanica, which I thought would do well in this richest county in the country (Montgomery) where many government employees and congressmen lived. They were the hardest to sell. This was a very distressing and depressing experience as I called on these wealthy homes.

When I came past the NIH hospital, I would stop and look up into the lighted windows and think of our little daughter lying there suffering and often hooked up to the many tubes giving her medication and life-giving blood or platelets. I don't recall crying out to God, "Why us?". Many other parents had children there, too, and they didn't have the comfort of knowing our Father in Heaven. I did question what God was doing in our lives. I thought of the times when I was troubled about my lack of feeling and compassion for the families of Navajo people who lost dear ones. Now I truly knew more of what they were experiencing. However, most of the time they grieved without hope, which made it even more difficult for them.

We had hoped that Mae would be able to get a better paying job than I, because she was an RN. However, she had to spend nearly every day at the hospital with Trudy. Pay was very low for nonprofessional work in that area. This added to our distress. Often, we didn't know where our next meal was coming from. Rice with a gravy made from chicken gizzards and hearts was our best buy. I recall Mae weeping at the clothesline, wondering where the money was coming from to make our next house payment. The next day a check came in the mail from Mae's home church. Also friends from the Washington, D. C. church as well as our neighbors would drop in with a few bags of groceries and the Rehoboth church also sent us a check. God was faithful in supplying our needs and we need not have worried.

Encouragements came from our sisters and brothers in the Lord in the Navajo churches too. John and Mary George were our assistants at the time. We were thrilled to get a tape made at the Tohlakai Church. Various members spoke of their loving concern and prayers for us. The group sang hymns in Navajo and English and some read encouraging scripture passages. Some of the people could hardly speak without weeping. The Navajo, contrary to many opinions, are an emotional and caring people. We learned this from Christian friends in the Shiprock CRC too, when they sent us a heart warming tape. We learned over and over again the value and love of the communion of saints.

Trudy had a partial remission a couple of times when she could be home and even go to school for a short time. We were always concerned that she might be injured while playing and have to be rushed to the hospital for blood. One time we had to rush her to the hospital when she got a sever allergic reaction while eating nuts and her throat began to swell so that she could hardly breath.

Mae had some interesting opportunities to witness her faith in Christ while visiting with parents of other sick children. Trudy was being treated on the children's floor for the treatment of cancer. Children came from many parts of the country with their parents. It was a traumatic experience for all of them, having to be uprooted from their homes and often separated from loved ones. Parents sat together in a solarium or lunch room exchanging experiences and often shedding tears together. We felt sorry for parents who didn't have faith in God and the resurrection promises of Christ. One mother said, "Our Mary won't have to go to purgatory because she suffered more than enough for her sins and maybe for some of her family." Mae said, "We don't believe in purgatory because the Bible says when Jesus died on the cross, He paid for all the sins of those who confess their sins and believe in Christ as Savior and Lord." The mother replied, "I wish I could believe that." We realized anew that only God can open hearts by His Word and Spirit.

When a child died and was missed by a friend, he or she would ask, "What happened to so and so?" Usually the parent or the nurses would say that the child went home or was moved to another floor. We thought it was best to be truthful so that slowly it would become a reality that death likely would occur. We didn't think it was wise or necessary for Trudy to face death early so she would have to dwell on it. We told the older children not to talk about it while Trudy was around. After we were in Maryland, the children were playing Monopoly and were asking around the board what each one would do with a thousand dollars if they had it. When it came to Trudy's turn, she said, "I would give it to the Red Cross, because I'm going to die anyway." The children didn't tell us this until after she died. She knew long before we talked to her about it that she would not live.

The doctors also said most of the children knew even though their parents wouldn't talk to them about it. Once when Trudy was suffering a lot of pain, she said she wished she could die. We asked her one evening, after her evening prayer, that if she died before she wakened, if she believed Jesus would take her to heaven. She said she believed in

Him and He would. We shed some tears together. At another time Mae and Trudy talked about death when a little friend was taken away and then Trudy's doctor said to tell her that they were doing all they could to find a cure.

We talked with parents who were losing an only child. That was almost more than they could bear. I recall the parents of one young man, around 15 years old sharing their hurt with us. The boy was playing football when his legs began to ache more than usual and when he was injured the bleeding wouldn't stop. His parents were devastated to find he had leukemia. They had pinned such high hopes on his future.

It was a sad sight to see so many boys and girls in the day rooms or walking through the halls with their intravenous poles receiving their life blood or platelets. Platelets are cells in the blood that cause clotting. To give them, the red cells are removed from the blood and the serum part of the blood is spun down so the platelets are concentrated in it. The red cells are often given back to the donor. Mae was able to give platelets for Trudy because they had the same blood type. At first they gave the whole plasma, but had to give so much that the patient sometimes went into congestive heart failure. This happened once to Trudy and she almost died.

When Trudy's illness became more and more critical, Social Services provided a Home-Maker to be with the children at home so Mae could be with Trudy and I could work. This lady would come around 10:30 AM and leave when I came home in the evening. She had dinner prepared when I came home. It was a wonderful service and she was with us for several weeks.

We didn't realize at the time how difficult it must have been for the other six children to live through these experiences. To complicate matters more, Sally became ill. The first symptoms were the same as Trudy's early symptoms: aching bones, petechiae, and later, a rash which turned out to be scarlet fever. Our pediatrician called Trudy's doctor at NIH to see if he would see Sally. In the end, they said her diagnosis was an atypical case of Rheumatic fever. We were so thankful it wasn't leukemia, but with the rheumatic fever, Sally had to stay out of school and a home school teacher came regularly to give her instruction.

We were prepared for Trudy's home-going, though it was difficult to see her gasp her last breath. We had her funeral in our supporting church in Jamestown, Michigan, and she was buried next to her grandmother in the Zutphen Cemetery near Jamestown.

After the funeral, Mae's folks went back to Maryland with us and spent a short time. I found a better job and we stayed there for several months and then went back to the work at Tohlakai. What a joy it was to be back with our friends there!

*Sweat lodge, heated with hot rocks.*

**Chapter X**

# SOME ENJOYABLE AND SOME DIFFICULT EXPERIENCES

*F*riends and relatives at times spoke of the sacrifices we made going to work far from home. We never thought so much of it as a sacrifice but as a privilege. The Lord gives blessings and rewards to compensate. However, children can suffer more than the parents because they are raised in isolation and often have to leave home to go to school long distances away. There were also compensations for the children. Now they can recall fond memories of unusual experiences. Under isolated conditions, our family developed a closeness others don't realize. We still benefit from that today. Of course, it helped that we had a large family.

At times, having a large family had its difficulties and pressures, especially for the mother, when the children or one of us became very ill. We had to go 130 miles to Rehoboth for medical care. I thanked the Lord over and over for Mae's ability as an R.N. and her calm spirit in times of emergencies which I shall tell of later. I want to say also that I am sure Mae experienced more of the burden of the work than I, having to spend so much time with the little ones alone and helping me with Ladies' Aid, extra cooking and baking for special occasions. I expected too much from her.

Speaking of Ladies' Aid meetings, we had some interesting and enjoyable times. When we were still at Shiprock, they worked diligently making quilts, selling them later to raise money for the church. They stitched away while we gave them God's Word and tried to get some discussions going. Someone usually brought baked goodies to have with coffee. We often missed out on the jovial conversations and laughter because of the language barrier.

One beautiful fall day, the ladies from Tohlakai packed lunches and together, we went about 30 miles west to the higher elevation just west of Window Rock, Arizona to pick up piñon nuts. Only trees about 7000 feet elevation produce nuts about every 4 years. Piñon nuts fall out of cones growing on an evergreen pine-like tree. The nuts are about the size of a large navy beans so it takes a lot of time and patience to pick them up by hand. If you don't have too much arthritic pain and stiffness, it is a rather pleasant pastime. The pine tree odors are pleasant. Then, there is a time of laughter when someone let's out an "ach." Accidently, a sheep dropping was mistakenly popped into the mouth and there was a soft crunch instead of the snap of a hard shell. Or occasionally, a stone was chomped on.

Gathering piñons was also a valuable source of income for some families. When we first came to the reservation, the nuts brought only 25 cents a pound but later $1.00 at trading posts. Many Navajo later packed them in small cellophane bags and sold them along the highways for a much better price. Some pinons were sold to the traders in 25# flour sacks. When it was melon, corn and squash harvest time they would take their produce, handmade jewelry and piñon nuts to the flea markets in the cities and towns bordering the reservation. Some also bring along the fixings for the delicious fried bread to sell along with coffee and mutton stew. The bread is fried on camp stoves on the tailgate of the pickup. The Navajo people are enterprising and very skillful with their hands. They produce beautiful paintings and artistic jewelry as well as rugs.

Another of the enjoyable times, which also gave us a break from the regular routine, were the annual Cottonwood Pass meetings. Those meetings were held high up on the Chuska Mountains, 13 miles west of Nahaschitti Mission. The higher altitude gave relief from the heat of the first two weeks of July. Christians came from most of our mission stations in the early days by wagon, horseback, and pickup. We all brought tents, cooking equipment and groceries. That was a time of Christian fellowship in song around the Word of God, brought by native and anglo missionaries under a huge tent. At first, most of the people sat on straw or pine needles on the ground or logs, but later more and more people brought folding chairs. It wasn't easy for us anglos to sit for 2 or 3 hours, morning, afternoon and evening, especially during the Navajo messages. We enjoyed seeing and hearing new Christians and older ones provide special music and give their testimonies. We saw these camp meetings as a means to encourage and strengthen Christians in their lives and faith. There were usually some conversions and recommitments during the ten day meetings.

We enjoyed meeting fellow missionaries from other areas and Navajo friends whom we had ministered to before and hadn't seen for a long time. These are joyous reunions. There were small tents pitched a distance from the large tent where Bible stories and activities for children were held. In the afternoon, the adults sometimes separated into groups where topics of their interests were discussed.

Young people had their activities in another area and had their own events such as volleyball, hikes, and soft ball. After the noon hour, the men got a soft ball game together or pitched horse shoes. I think the ladies sat around the campfire and visited and took care of the babies. That aspect wasn't so nice because the small children easily got dirty in the black mountain soil or in the mud around the spring. Pampers weren't known and when you had one or two little ones in diapers it aggravated the situation. It wasn't a pleasant time for Mae.

The nights got pretty cold up in that high altitude and the children became uncovered and began crying, one after the other, which didn't help to give parents composure. We usually awakened before sunrise with someone nearby chopping wood for the breakfast fire. It felt so good to warm up around an early pine or piñon fire and smell bacon frying and coffee brewing. I made pancakes often to satisfy the ravenous appetites of the growing brood. We would take a hike at times to some high rocky point where we could get a panoramic view of the hot scorched earth far out in the distance. We knew we would have to descend again into the oven before long. However, at times we received some early flash floods. When that happened tenting wasn't so comfortable and the adobe roads, if they could be called roads, became impassable. We all helped each other weather the storm and get through the mud holes.

Nearly every summer or fall, each of the mission stations held their camp meetings and announced the events in the churches over the radio. This gave the Christians an opportunity to work together, planning the program, choosing the special speakers and butchering sheep which they donated. Even young beef was brought at times. This big event was held under an outdoor shelter built by the church members. This shade (Cha' ha' oh) was built near the church and consisted of a frame made of poles hauled down from a nearby, or not so near, mountain. The frame was covered with branches from the cottonwood trees which grew along the arroyos and on mountain tops. Usually a platform was built by the men and the church piano brought in. So a lot of work and planning went into the occasion. We felt it served as a good substitute for the social life of the traditional summer and fall native ceremonies such as squaw dances.

A lot of pressure was put to bear on many Christians by well meaning relatives to take part in the ceremonies performed by the medicine man for a sick relative. People came for miles around to the Christian Camp meetings as well as to the native healing ceremonies. As more and more of the Navajo became educated and took on the anglo culture, the ceremonies, according to older Navajo, became more and more places of revelry and drunkenness. We thought the Christian Camp Meetings were uncomfortably long but the native rites were all night affairs! I think our wonderful Lord and Savior should receive as much or more honor? He not only heals the sick but comforts the afflicted and gives joy to the sin burdened soul by forgiving him all his transgressions. Small wonder that the hills rang with his praise! And the trees of the field clapped their hands!

An unusual and sad thing happened a short distance from our Teec Nos Pos Mission at one of those squaw dances. I was home alone with the children that night. The children were in bed already when I heard a knock at the back door. A couple of men were standing there near their wagon. I wondered what they could want at this late hour. One of them could speak pretty good English. He said, "We would like to have you call the hospital in Shiprock for us." I invited them in the house and asked them what the problem was. The older man said, "I killed a man." I said, "Killed a man? Where is he?" He led me to his wagon and showed me a body lying under an old army blanket. He had a huge welt behind one ear. I asked, "What happened?" He said, "This man was drinking at the dance and became unruly and was causing fights. I tried to stop him and in the scuffle kicked him behind the ear by accident." I called the Navajo police in Shiprock. It took about an hour for them to come. I felt a little uncomfortable carrying on a conversation with someone who had just committed murder. The FBI questioned me concerning this death. The man was acquitted.

I want to tell of another difficult experience. One night about midnight we heard a loud knock on our back door. There stood an acquaintance with a look of alarm and fear. He said excitedly, "Come quickly, my wife is dying! Hurry, I need help." I told him to go back home and I would come as soon as I had gotten dressed. I knew the lady was pregnant and thought she might be having a miscarriage. I figured I had better take my smoother riding station wagon instead of the rough riding pickup on the rocky road.

As soon as I stopped near the closest hogan, Mr. Jonas came out and said, "Hurry, come in and help me. My wife is dying." I stepped in and saw the lady lying on the dirt floor on a sheepskin. Her eyes were rolled back in her head. Mr. Jonas and I picked her up as carefully as we could and placed her on the back seat.

The husband sat with Lilly, holding her head in his lap. I thought of the recent times the couple had been coming to church with their little children and looked forward to the time Lilly would confess her new found faith in the Lord Jesus and be baptized.

After we had gone a rugged ten miles and neared Biclabito, Mr. Jonas said in a trembling voice, "Mr. Kruis, I believe my wife just died." I decided we should go on to the Public Health Hospital in Shiprock, another twenty long, rocky miles. I was thankful the fall rains had stopped so the deep arroyos wouldn't be torrents of muddy water to hold us up.

When we arrived in Shiprock, we carried the body into the old wood frame hospital. After examining the body, the doctor said, "We had better notify the police. It looks as if someone has beaten and strangled her." Then the lady's sister, who had ridden with us, said, "He did it." Pointing at Mr. Jonas. The Navajo police came from the nearby police station and took Frank away. The trip back home was the longest thirty miles I had ever ridden. After taking Lilly's sister to her home, I went home to have breakfast with my family.

The prisoner was later moved to a more distant town for fear of a reprisal by family members. The FBI was in charge of the investigation, since the murder was committed on Federally supervised land. The natives are still considered wards of the U.S. government and still receive many benefits given at the time when treaties were signed.

Mr. Jonas claimed that he had been eating peyote the evening before the death of his wife. He had been having some health problems and had been told that the peyote would be good for him. (At the time peyote was outlawed on the reservation.) Mr. Jonas said he didn't know what he was doing because of the hallucinations. I thought we should make a court case of the incident so that the peyote would possibly remain outlawed. I went to see a lawyer in Gallup to get his opinion. He told me it would be a very difficult and expensive case because there wasn't enough information and it still wasn't declared a drug. We didn't pursue it any further.

Later I was subpoenaed to appear at the grand jury trial in Tucson, Arizona. Three members of Lilly's family rode the 400 miles with me to Tucson for the trial. To say the least, it was a very sad and quite tense trip.

I learned something interesting and clever from the elderly gentleman with us. I wondered why he carried a woman's purse under his arm. He used this purse when he paid his bills. It was a decoy in case of a robbery. The larger amount of cash was kept safely in his pocket billfold.

Mr. Jonas pleaded guilty and received quite a lengthy jail term but was released early due to good behavior.

Enjoyable and rewarding experiences on the field were the times I worked with the young people. In the beginning most of the activity was done in the summer months because nearly all the young people were gone to off reservation government boarding schools for nine months. We corresponded with a few of them. Some of them wrote back to us but had a hard time expressing themselves. Their English was so limited. At times, we came to homes where letters had been received from their boarding school kids. We were asked to read them and the interpreter would tell the parents what the letter said. When I received a letter, it usually ended with a request to say a big fat 'Hello' to the folks or to say a big fat 'Hello' to the people in church.

It was difficult and sad for the parents to see their children off as they boarded busses, lined up at the trading posts or other centers. We saw hugs, kisses and tears. There were also tragic experiences we heard of and knew about when boys (I can't recall instances of girls) ran away from school because they hated it or got very lonesome. They didn't seem to care how cold it was when they started out hiking across country alone or with a friend. Some have died of exposure and others lost toes due to frost bite. The schools have been sued for allowing the child to 'escape', but I don't see how they could prevent it all the time. Parents wouldn't want children to feel like they were in a penitentiary either. The parents in one case were awarded a large sum of money resulting from a lawsuit.

Indian General Conference, an organization similar to Classis, annually appointed a committee to arrange for a day's outing for Young People at one of the posts or a mountain top. There were committees to arrange recreation events, a song leader, and an inspirational speaker. I recall starting out early in the morning to pick up young people at there homes. There was always a contest to see which mission could bring the largest group. We did our best to get a good number and usually were successful. We could get young people to go who didn't come to church. I felt they could benefit by seeing that Christians could have fun and we hoped some would accept Christ as Savior at the inspirational meeting.

I also did a lot of work with the Young People whenever and wherever I could because I knew they were the future of the church and I wanted to help them have something to do to hopefully keep them out of mischief. Winter activity included taking kids up to McGaffey Lake ice fishing, tubing for those who were brave enough, and ice skating.

At one time, I advertised for ice skates and many people responded, so we had skates to use. We built a fire out on the ice for a wiener roast. Our boys always enjoyed the outings along with the Indian kids. When at Tohlakai we went sledding and pulled children on a discarded car hood behind the pickup through the fields. What fun and excitement! Pop and wieners were the usual fare.

I got irritated when interpreters took their small children along to the youth meetings. I suggested in the kindest ways possible that they didn't fit in with the older youth. One interpreter said, "Don't they (young kids) need Jesus too?" I thought that in the native culture perhaps a distinction wasn't made between ages for activities or religious events.

Where we had enough young people, I formed a soft ball and volley ball team. At times, we competed with those from other posts and had fellowship in church afterwards.

When we had annual youth meetings at Rehoboth, we would get home near midnight and were worn out. One time while returning with a full pickup, I fell asleep and woke up in time to swerve to avoid hitting a bridge.

One summer Paul Redhouse and I arranged to have his young people from Red Valley meet with our Teec Nos Pos young people under some cottonwood trees halfway between our posts. It was a scenic spot. Mae's sister, Helen, was visiting us at the time and went along to play the little portable pump organ. We had a rousing good song-fest there among the beautiful redrocks. We ended the time with a luscious watermelon bust and marshmallow roast.

Seeking the lost took us up into the nearby mountains over rugged trails to visit the people living in their summer homes. Most of the people had a summer home where they lived while pasturing their herds where the weather was cooler and there was usually more grass. We also visited them in the fall during piñon nut harvest time and brought the Gospel by hand wound record players. We were able to get the players and Navajo language recordings through Gospel Recordings, Inc. We also left these players in homes where new converts would use them to learn the catechism. In those days, they had to memorize the answers to one hundred nine questions.

They also learned and enjoyed the Navajo hymns as well as Christian messages from the records. The records and needles didn't last long due to rugged use and dusty conditions. The player was called a 'singing metal' and the telephone 'talking metal' in Navajo. I always enjoyed having those regular Bible lessons because it gave us a time of close spiritual fellowship and to get really well acquainted. I tried and usually visited the Christian families before communion every three months. This was also an enjoyable exchange. Sometimes family problems surfaced and were dealt with.

**Natural spires in the Land of Enchantment.**

## Chapter XI

# OUR CONTACT WITH MORMONISM

At first, when we came to the field we seldom saw Mormon missionaries, but as time went along there were more and more of them seeking to convert people to their faith. There later sprung up many kinds of faiths to the confusions of the Navajo, who would ask, "Who can we believe? You all tell us you are right and yet you claim to believe in one God." It wasn't an easy question to answer. I tried to answer as honestly and scripturally as possible. I told them that the Holy Bible was the only true guide for our faith and life. They could only know God through faith in His Son, Jesus and forgiveness of sin through His shed blood. We explained that the denominations were like a wagon wheel. The spokes represent different denominations and the hub is Christ and Him crucified. The Holy Spirit would reveal the truth to them if they asked Him and studied God's Word diligently.

We could spot Mormon missionaries anywhere by their white shirts and black ties. They were very friendly and looked so clean cut. When we met them at the trading post they were extra friendly and wanted to shake hands. They wanted the Navajo to accept them as one of 'us.' It took a while for them to be accepted on the reservation. Those young men and sometimes a couple young women, just out of high school, were expected to give two years of 'mission' and then go back to school or some career. It made us a little angry that they would brag about how they volunteered their time and we worked for wages. They tell people that the other churches have lost the real truths given by God and that the Bible is God's Word, but not complete. Therefore, God raised up Joseph Smith to give him new revelations by the visions he had from the angel Moroni and also that Joseph Smith found gold plates buried in the ground in New York. These plates were written in some old Egyptian language, which Joseph Smith translated by means of the Urim and Thummim, such as the Old Testament priests had.

Others of their prophets later received more messages which contradict the Holy Scriptures. One of their main teachings is that, "Just as God is we shall become, and as we are God once was." This means that if men (not women) keep all the covenants and ordinances, tithes, etc., and are married in the Mormon Temple, they will be Gods in the third heaven. Their's is a work of righteousness. They claim they believe in Christ's saving grace, but we find that they add a lot of `must do'.

This religion appeals to people because it is the nature of man to take upon himself some righteousness and good and the more he does good, the better he feels and better his standing is with God, instead of receiving Christ and His saving work on the cross as our only righteousness. The Mormons also allow for the heathen gods, since there are many gods, therefore, the religious ceremonies of the natives can be useful. Thus, they compromise.

The Mormons also teach that their's is the true religion because they alone have the Melchisedek priesthood, the priesthoods, the prophets and all the Old Testament offices as well as those of the New Testament.

When serving at Teec Nos Pos, the Mormon traders were coming quite regularly to our church services and mid-week Bible Classes. When Mormon leaders from Kirtland got wind of this, they told them they had to come to their own church for instruction. They still came to our mid-week classes but less regularly. They said, "We would like you to visit our class sometime. We are taught the same things but it is said a little differently."

I knew very little about the Mormon religion, so out of courtesy to the traders and to be able to witness more intelligently to the Mormons, I decided to go.

It was with an uneasy feeling that I went. At first the congregation met, then we split up in classes. There were about thirty-five adults in our class. The leader gave a lesson consisting mostly of questions pertaining to their doctrines. He asked what certain texts meant. He would look over at me occasionally. Finally, he asked if anyone had a question or anything to say. I said that I didn't quite agree with one of the statements or possibly didn't understand. Then the leader asked if I would like to come and speak to the group. (Wow, what an opportunity!) However, it was a little scary. I knew the Mormons could really put the pressure on and I would be standing before 'highpriests'. Rev. Henry Evenhouse was visiting on the field at the time. I asked him if he thought it was presumptive for me to do such a thing. He said, "Go ahead, if you think you can handle it."

After praying about it, I decided to accept the challenge and asked the Lord to lead me to choose the right passage. I chose the passage from Hebrews 7:26-28, about the High priesthood of Jesus and His complete sacrifice. After the message I opened the session for questions. I received some good responses. One question I recall was, "What do you mean by being washed in the blood?" The Holy Spirit gave me the words to speak and the courage I requested. All honor belongs to God.

I found through the years that it is so difficult for me not to get in an argument with Mormons. I know it does no good, and it causes harm. It is so difficult to be patient when the Scriptures are so falsely represented.

I have tried to read the "Book of Mormon" and did read a lot of their literature. Little did I know that later, my son, Dan, would accept a call to go to Salt Lake City to pastor a church and work with other pastors to bring the Gospel. The Lord blessed their work there. They have seen some Mormons turn to the Lord and join their church.

Another interesting thing happened while living in Gallup after my retirement. One day, a couple of young elders came to my door. I didn't care to be interrupted at the time and told them so. One of the men said, "You asked us to come." "No, I didn't," I said. I thought to myself, "They are trying one of their tricks to get their foot in the door". I told them so. "We can prove it," they said. Then they went out to their pickup and came back. They said, "See? Your signature is on this paper, asking us to stop and see you." I examined the signature. It was not mine. It was my son, Brian's. He had visited the Mormon tabernacle in Salt Lake City and signed a form requesting a visit. He wanted to learn more about Mormonism and wanted to challenge the elders to accept the Gospel of Salvation by grace. Brian met nearly every week for 10 sessions with the young men to discuss intently their opposing views. Brian really dug earnestly into the Word trusting the Holy Spirit to do His work of conversion. I admire Brian's patience and persistence. Only eternity will reveal the results.

*That They Might Know*

It always makes me sad to see some of the Navajo children go to the Mormon religious instruction classes on released time, even though they had much fewer children than we did. We find that so few people realize that the Mormon faith is absolutely false and unscriptural. The elders are clever in their presentation, beginning with a pleasant approach and presenting Biblical doctrines and then coming out with the "Book of Mormon" and its teachings. An appealing aspect of their faith is their emphasis on the family life. They also teach opposition to the use of alcohol, tobacco and coffee. They want to be accepted as Christians in the religious arena. And while the Mormon traders are opposed to the use of alcohol, tobacco and coffee, they will sell it for profit in their stores.

While in a Navajo home, a young lady once asked me if it was wrong to drink coffee. She said, "The Mormon elders said it would turn the inside of your stomach black." The girl's mother was present too and I knew the Navajo people usually drink a lot of coffee. The mother was listening intently for my answer. I said, "The Bible is our guide in matters of living the Christian life pleasing to God, but the Bible has nothing to say about coffee because apparently they didn't have coffee in those days. However, some people can't drink coffee because of some ailment they have and coffee would do them harm. Doctors may prohibit it in some cases. If a person believes it is wrong to drink coffee or any other thing, he shouldn't do it and sin against his or her conscience or his or her religious belief."

A family once asked me to participate with Mormon elders at a funeral. This, I did, so as not to offend the family, and to bring the Gospel message. However, it was an uncomfortable situation. I still recall the scene at a family burial ground with huge white feathery snowflakes floating down from the sky.

On one occasion two young "elders" came to my interpreter's door. He let them in. During their stay, they told John that if he accepted the Mormon religion and obeyed the covenants and teachings, he could go to heaven and become a white man. John answered, "Who wants to be a white man?" Before they left, they asked if they could give their personal testimony (which they try to get in so they can leave on a positive note). One of the men said he had gone or been a member of different protestant churches, but God led him to the Mormon faith. John answered, "That can't be, God wouldn't lead a person away from His Word." I thought that was an excellent answer.

To gain more insight into the Mormon religion, my son Brian and I once attended a Sunday afternoon meeting in a Mormon church here in Gallup.

*One of New Mexico's scenic rock formations.*

## Chapter XII

# TOADLENA

We had been serving the Lord at Tohlakai (Bethlehem Chapel) for five years on our second term there when we were asked by the Home Board to work at Toadlena. We figured it would be good for the work at Tohlakai and for us to have a change. I felt quite burned out there. Toadlena is thirteen miles off highway 666 about 70 miles north of Gallup.

The children loved the countryside in the foot hills of the beautiful Chuska mountains. There was a deep canyon where they often went to play and build a dam in a small stream. The children could go to school about 12 miles away on a school bus. This school went to 6th grade. Rick and Dan went to boarding school at Rehoboth. When it came time for Bob and Ed to go to Rehoboth they had a difficult time being away from home. They had to stay in the basements of missionaries homes and eat in the dining room.

The work at Toadlena wasn't easy. We had to deal with some serious family problems and at the same time do all the campwork we could. I have always tried to maintain a schedule of three days of campwork a week and take care of the released time teaching children in the government schools. We had an active ladies aid, midweek prayer meeting, and Bible study, and during the summer, weekly youth meetings. Sundays were busy, having worship services at Toadlena mornings and evenings and in the afternoon in an old vacated schoolhouse thirteen miles east at Newcomb.

One thing that made the work difficult was having interpreters who weren't very qualified. I found out one man was jealous of my leadership and would speak evil of me behind my back. I had to let him go. Satan always does all he can to hinder the Lord's work. This drove us to our knees pleading for God's grace and wisdom.

While we were at Toadlena, a beautiful new church building was built and dedicated with great joy. Ted Tibboel came up from Rehoboth to build the church with what local help we could muster. We were thankful to have indoor toilets and kitchen facilities for special occasions. There were folding doors, too, so we could have classrooms in back. I taught an adult Sunday School class while the interpreter gave the message in Navajo.

While we were at Toadlena, there was a large celebration to which the church and community came. It was to celebrate the 50th wedding anniversary of Mr. and Mrs. Louis Cambridge. It was held in the summer shelter. The ladies of the church fixed a delicious meal of fried bread, mutton stew and roasted ribs plus a lot of other food and a huge tiered wedding cake. After the meal, we sang hymns and heard testimonies.

A sad thing happened later. A father in a home near the mission was an alcoholic and created family problems and even violence at times. One Saturday, the wife came to our house and asked if she could stay a while for fear of getting beaten. After some time, I told her I would go with her to her home to see what could be done. She had padlocked the door on the small house and this was broken. We looked around to see if we could find the man. Soon we saw him lying on the ground a little ways from the house under a piñon tree. There was a .22 caliber rifle and an empty whiskey bottle lying next to him. We discovered to our sorrow that the man had shot himself in the forehead. He was still breathing. We got a blanket out of the house and covered him and then went back to the mission to call the Navajo Police in Shiprock.

It seemed like an eternity for them to come with an ambulance. They asked the circumstances and took pictures and then brought him to Shiprock. From there, they flew him to Albuquerque. He lived thirty days with the bullet lodged in the back of his skull. It was a very difficult time for the mother and the six children. The mother was a confessing Christian and had a Christian burial for her husband but his relatives weren't Christians, so they wanted to have some native rites. They tried to find the man's horse so they could bring it to the grave and kill it there so it could be used by the deceased in later life. We were glad they couldn't find the horse. The family was poor and could make use of the horse or sell it. The relatives did bring his saddle, cut it up and buried it with the coffin. It took a very long time for the mother to recover from this traumatic experience. We are glad to say that her oldest son had accepted the Lord as his Savior and today is serving as an assistant in a Navajo Baptist Church in Gallup. Her daughter is the wife of one of our native pastors now serving at Toadlena. Other family members are also living for the Lord. Praise His Name!

The old school building we used at Newcomb for our Sunday afternoon services had to be heated with wood or coal and when one of our Navajo members didn't get there early to build a fire, it took a long time to get the large room warm. We stood or sat in a circle around the stove, but our backs stayed cold. Mae's hands were almost too cold to play the piano but the warmth of the Christian fellowship made it all worth while. The roof leaked in places so we had fresh water on the floor in pools after rain. We had to use an outhouse. At the time of this writing, the members at Newcomb are using a large house trailer for meetings and have a church building under construction and it's quite a ways finished. Many go to the Toadlena church for morning worship and special meetings.

One of the enjoyable things at Toadlena was the time spent with the family fishing and swimming in the nearby small reservoirs. On one occasion, a rainstorm came up suddenly over the mountain while we were swimming. Pretty soon it turned into a severe hail storm. The sky was suddenly black as night and wind was blowing furiously. The three of us, shivering cold, took what shelter there was under a small olive tree. When our skin began to turn blue with cold, I decided to run for help to a neighbor some distance away who had a four wheeler sitting in his yard. Fortunately, he was home and came to our rescue. We were thankful to get back home to a warm shelter.

On another occasion when I was up at the trading post getting mail, a Navajo man by the name of Walter Upshaw said, "Mr. Kruis, does your family enjoy eating fish?" I said, "Yes, we surely do. Why?" "Well then," he said, "Go get your sons and some burlap bags and we'll go down to Captain Tom Lake and catch some." I thought, "Now what's this Indian up to? What's the trick?" When we got down to the small lake (a reservoir, actually), we saw that it was going dry. The Navajo below the dam had drained the lake nearly dry to irrigate their small farms. The summer had been very dry and not much snow had fallen on the Chuska Mountain range that winter to feed into the lake.

We followed Mr. Upshaw's instructions and waded out into the gooey mud and water up to our waists. It was summer so the water was warm. We could see fish moving around with their fins sticking out of the water. So we all got in a big circle and drove the fish toward the center and caught a large number of them in our bags. We never realized there were so many large fish in there, though we had fished there. We caught about 8 six pound small mouth bass and some good sized rainbow trout. We cleaned the fish and put them in our freezer and had fish a long time. The bass had a lot of fat along the backbone, so we became a little tired of that fish.

One experience on campwork stands out in my mind. My interpreter and I went in our pickup to quite a high hill overlooking a camp below. We could see a fire burning outside near the home so we knew there must be someone around. We wound our way down a narrow gravel path and soon met the family outside. This McDonald family had been coming to church with grandma Bigman quite regularly. We sat around the fire over which delicious smelling lamb ribs were roasting. I uttered a prayer silently, asking for a message to bring.

As I saw the lamb ribs roasting, the message came to me to present Jesus, the lamb of God. I first told them how the foods we eat were all living at one time but had to die so we could live. The lamb had to bleed and die so they could live by eating the flesh. This led into the message of Isaiah 53 and John's message, "Behold the Lamb of God, who takes away the sins of the world." What a joy it was to hear Mrs. McDonald testify that she wanted this Lord to be her Savior and confess Him in church. As we taught her the Bible lessons in preparation for her public confession and church membership, the husband and older children showed real interest. Later, Mr. McDonald also confessed the Lord as his Savior. We praised the Lord that we could reap harvests where Rev. J.C. Kobes and others had planted and watered in the Toadlena area.

We had black, white and red races in our services at Toadlena. Teachers came from the boarding school. We even had a wedding for one couple. It was a joy for us to have Mrs. Alice Watchman and her adult children come to church when they were home from boarding school. We became acquainted with Alice when she came to church at Teec Nos Pos.

After leaving the McDonald home, we took a little used trail through rock strewn wash. We could see that water had gushed through here often during the sudden cloudbursts. We picked our way carefully with our pickup to dodge the huge rocks, so we wouldn't hit the oil pan and really be stranded. The trail led us past some huge cottonwood trees clothed in shimmering gold fall colors. The sky was clear blue dotted with clouds.

We came to a tar paper covered house where the Yazzie family lived. We wondered how this large family could possibly live in such a small two bedroom house. The mother was a confessing Christian and the father had confessed the Lord at one time but was quite a heavy drinker now. As we approached the door two scrawny dogs got up, yawned, and with a dull look ambled off. We knocked on the homemade door and heard the call, 'tin' (come in). Mrs. Yazzie offered us a bench alongside a large homemade table. When we noticed she was fixing some tortilla dough to bake on the top of the kitchen range, we suggested we come back some other time. She said, "Please stay." As she flip-flopped the tortilla from hand to hand, we watched in amazement as her little bright eyed four year old daughter did the same thing with her little ball of dough. After flopping the dough back and forth and pulling it outward it became beautifully round and flat. Then it was placed on the hot stove or could be fried in deep fat. This fried bread is delicious and makes an excellent meal with roast mutton or mutton stew.

Mrs. Yazzie didn't look at us directly as she carried on some small talk. We noticed when she turned that she was trying to hide a swollen cheek and black eye. She began to cry and amidst her tears said, "Mr. Kruis, I don't know how long I can take this anymore. My husband is drinking more and more and is getting meaner to me and the children. I know the Bible says it is wrong to have a divorce, but what must I do? I am sorry for my children. They love their father when he is sober, but he seldom comes home that way anymore. He is gone a lot. What must I do?"

We had encouraged Mr. Yazzie to get treatment at the Friendship House in Gallup. He said it didn't help. He always said he could quit if he really tried. I said I would advise her to get a separation for a while.

Later, while riding in my car, I heard a preacher on the radio say that a person who no longer loves his wife and doesn't care for her is committing adultery because he is cutting off his relationship with her. He likened it to Israel whom God said was committing fornication when they were unfaithful to Him. I could buy that. Mrs. Yazzie did get a divorce later on after we left that area of work. She also told me that she often had to leave the small children alone so she could get water from a well or herd her small flock of sheep. We thought of another home where we saw a four or five year old girl building a fire in her home on a very cold day and taking care of a small baby. We often wondered what would happen in an emergency when the mother was away and the father was gone to work on the Santa Fe railroad for months at a time. Our hearts went out to these dear people.

## Chapter XIII

# A DIFFICULT DECISION.

**H**ow could we think of leaving the Land of Enchantment and our Navajo people considering the deep attachments we have? It came about in this way while serving at Toadlena. We had been there for only two and a half years and yet felt led by the Lord to make this move in response to a call from the Faith Christian Reformed Church in Holland, Michigan. They asked if we would consider an appointment to pastor a small country church near South Haven, Michigan. When we were told that there were four other men being considered, we decided to be interviewed by the committee by phone as they proposed. We decided if it was the Lord's will that we move to Michigan, we would get the appointment. It would be His appointment. It was like putting out a fleece. Other factors entered the picture too. Before we came to Toadlena, we were told there were problems in the church among the members. We didn't find out until we moved there how serious they were. My interpreter found it very difficult to explain the personal problems in the congregational meetings.

My supervisor, Rev. Paul Redhouse, came out from Teec Nos Pos to help with a couple of the meetings. When we received the request from Faith Church, things were pretty well settled but we knew there would be scars and one family did leave the church. We felt it would perhaps be better if a new pastor who hadn't been involved took over if the Lord led in that direction. Another factor that we considered was that three of our boys had to room and board at Rehoboth, which was 75 miles away. Two of the boys found the adjustment very difficult and distressing. One of them threatened to run away.

When I was interviewed by phone two questions were emphasized:
1. What is your position regarding church discipline?
2. What is your position on open or close communion?
After we arrived in South Haven, we realized the reason for the questions and experienced the difficulties of dealing with the situation that existed.

We left Toadlena on New Years Eve, 1969. As we stopped briefly in front of the beautiful new church building with the red and green floodlights lighting up the white steeple (installed for Christmas), we had mixed feelings of sorrow and anticipation.

The long trip to Michigan in midwinter had its scary times as we traveled long hours over snowy roads with our six children and pulling a large luggage trailer. We always gave thanks to our heavenly Father for His watchful care over us as we traveled many, many miles across country to visit Mae's parents in Washington State and to Michigan to visit my folks. On this trip, we were stopped late one night in a small town by a traffic officer telling us the tail lights on our trailer weren't working. The officer followed us to a motel where we had to hole up until we could get the problem fixed the next day.

When we arrived in South Haven, Michigan, one of the boys said, "Where are the mountains?" The huge sand dunes on the shores of Lake Michigan were the only semblance of mountains near by. We all would miss the beautiful Chuska mountains at Toadlena and the rugged rock formations. The gloomy winter days were difficult to adjust to, but before long, the kids were enjoying the snow for sledding and the ice pond about a mile away for skating. Later in the summer, this pond was an enjoyable swimming hole for them and friends.

Kibbie Corners had once been a busy community with a store, a pickle processing plant, a railroad and spur, and a Farmer's Grange Hall. The only things left now were an old store building used at this time for a dwelling and the Grange Hall next to it. The Grange Hall was turned over to the community for a church. The basement had been used for recreation for youth. The Faith church had permission to conduct the worship services and church activities there. The former lay pastor lived in Holland, but now due to more intensive and extensive evangelism in the community the church asked us to live at Kibbie. We agreed that would be better. They asked us if we were willing to live in the large church basement if they put in partitions for living quarters. We did this for about 6 months until we could find our own housing, a house bought at Hawkhead. It was a country crossroad with a large old vacated general store on our lot, a Town Hall still used occasionally, and one farm house. This was a rather unique country situation. It was like living on the edge of 'old times'.

It wasn't easy for the children to begin a new semester in schools in South Haven. Dan was quite bitter about having to leave the basketball team on which he played at Rehoboth. It was against the rules to join the South Haven team until he resided at least a semester in that county. Bob and Ed did well on the swim team during the next semester until graduation. Bob went to the State meet.

The area was largely a fruit farming community. There was a nice group of adults and youth on Sundays and for youth activities during the week. It was a plus that we had our children and youth attending church and young peoples' gatherings. I have always enjoyed working with the youth and participated as much as I could in their sports, etc. Our church attendance grew and the Lord blessed His work with some professions of faith and conversions. The Faith church supervised the work and sent help in the way of Sunday School teachers and Daily Vacation Bible School help. We appreciated their work of love and our good relationship with the Evangelism Committee and pastor, the Rev. Charles Steenstra. Most Sunday evenings, we attended the Hope Reformed church in South Haven where we developed long lasting friendships. We also enjoyed the Fellowship meetings of about nine lay pastors and their wives who had chapels in the larger area. To this day, we enjoy meeting these friends out here in New Mexico.

While teaching a catechism class, and after a discussion with the young people and a lot of study, I came to the conclusion that one of the doctrines of the church was unscriptural. I felt I could no longer teach it so I decided to tell the Evangelism Committee that I could no longer pastor the Kibbie Church and be honest to my conviction. With reluctance, they accepted my resignation.

While we were still working on the Indian Field, I was having a lot of headaches. Our doctor said they were due to tension. I still experienced them in Michigan and thought they might go away if I did secular work, but that didn't help. We later found out that I had pinched nerves between the vertebrae in my neck. Tension did aggravate the problem.

A friend of ours who had just begun selling real estate visited us one evening and out of the blue said, "What will you take for your house? I think I can get so much for it." The price was more than we paid for it so we said go ahead and try it. About the same, time we saw an ad in THE BANNER, our church paper requesting a registered nurse and a dietary supervisor in the Rehoboth Hospital. While prayerfully considering that ad, Mr. Baylor, the real estate man said he had a prospective buyer for a little less than he had mentioned. Would we sell for the price offered? We called the administrator of the hospital and both Mae and I were offered jobs. Mae had been working for a doctor in South Haven. He was also leaving and I decided to quit the boat building job at Chris Craft in Holland. We decided to accept the offers and leave.

With the profit from the house, we were able to make a good down payment on our present house in Gallup. Our missionary friend, Stan Siebersma, arranged for us to rent a small two bedroom house at Ft. Wingate. At least we had temporary shelter though it was a little crowded to say the least. We enjoyed the fellowship in the Ft. Wingate church and continued going there for a long time.

Bob was in twelfth grade and Ed in the eleventh when we decided to return to New Mexico. They wanted to finish school in South Haven. John and Marilyn Bright, members of the Reformed Church in South Haven, offered to have Bob and Ed live with them. We were glad to pay their room and board. The boys enjoyed living there but came home for the summers. We were thankful, and are to this day, for the Christian influence these good friends had on our sons.

The Rehoboth Hospital hired me to be the dietary supervisor, but when I went to work I was told the dietary supervisor decided to stay. I was hired to be the first shift cook which turned out for the best because it was a good experience to learn dietary cooking and observe supervisory work in the dietary department. After sometime, the supervisor left and I took her place. I had almost all Navajo help which gave me opportunities to witness for Christ.

While working in the hospital, I had Sundays off. I could continue to go to Fence Lake to preach on Sunday afternoons in a small country church 66 miles south of Gallup. The congregation was made up largely of cattle ranchers who were from many different denominational backgrounds. This was an interesting experience. I went out there some Saturdays to get acquainted with the people in their homes. The ranches were large often having from one to three sections. One of the ranchers, a Mr. Brown, came faithfully to build the fire in the wood burning stove in the center of the adobe stuccoed building. It was a beautiful drive going through part of the Zuni reservation. After three years, we decided it was too wearing. We got a Christian man from Gallup to take our place.

While working at the hospital, I was asked from time to time to preach in one of our churches which I gladly did. When Pastor Stan Siebersma decided to leave the pastoral work at Navajo, New Mexico, I was asked by the Regional Home Missionary, Rev. Dykema to take up the work. It was supposed to be a temporary position but lasted three years. At first, I just held Sunday morning services and a mid-week prayer and Bible Study. After I retired from the dietary supervisory work, I got permission to spend two afternoons a week visiting homes in the village of Navajo in addition to the other services.

The Navajo tribe rented a former post office building to use for a legal arrangement of $1 a year. It was a metal building with a knotty pine interior. The church group fixed up the interior to make an attractive meeting place with good facilities.

The Lord blessed His Word to bring in new families. The nucleus was made up of three stable families whose men were Rehoboth graduates. Most of the people in the community worked at the local lumber mill and were English speaking, so we didn't need an interpreter. It was really a joy to work with this congregation and in the community. One of the young women, a Rehoboth graduate named Irene Curley, led the children's church and another, Linda Henio, played the piano for the services. A retired Navajo missionary and wife were an encouragement.

One special experience stands out in my mind. I visited a middle aged man in a small cabin a short distance just south of the village. Benny soon asked us to pick him up for church. At first, someone had to carry him and place him in a car or pickup because as a result of accidents, he became partially paralyzed and had to have his legs amputated. As time went on Benny opened his heart to the Lord and wanted to be baptized. We spent many hours together studying God's Word. We worked together on learning to read Navajo and singing some Navajo songs. I was glad there was no one around to hear us sing most of the time. An older sister listened often as we went through the catechism so we had the opportunity to teach her the way of salvation too. She never did confess the Lord as her Savior before she suddenly passed away.

A couple of doctors, who were friends of the Rehoboth church, had a van which they had used for taking their handicapped father places. After their father passed away, they gave the van to us at Navajo so we could run Benny's wheelchair into it on a ramp. The men of our church took turns picking Benny up for church.

Things got real tough for Benny at times when no one was around to help fire the stove, get a meal or take care of him in other ways. I always enjoyed being with Benny. His cheerfulness was an inspiration. When I had a tendency to complain of arthritic aches in my legs, I would think of Benny who had no legs, but didn't complain.

After serving at Navajo (a 44 mile trip) for three years, a young Christian Navajo from Window Rock, Arizona took over the challenge to take my place. He was an elder in his church at Window Rock and a tribal judge. Tom Tso was willing to work in this 'tent making' ministry on a part time basis as I had done. Tom was later elevated to Chief Justice in the tribe which made him extra busy. At this writing, he has resigned from church work.

I just hope the Home Mission Board sees the challenge of the needy work and its good prospects for growth and sends a full time pastor. It seems to me that the field is ripe unto harvest. A new high school has been built there in addition to their large elementary school. It is one of the largest communities in which our churches are located and has more opportunity for a stable economy and growth. I marvel at the way the young men there are taking leadership with their limited training.

We are always anxious to hear news from our many friends in the Land of Enchantment. The Christian Indian paper helps us keep in touch and we are always looking for our friends to stop in at 221 Verdi D. in Gallup.

At this time, I have been distributing New Testaments to four large truck stops on I-40. About forty a week are picked up by the truckers. I also have the opportunity to visit with truckers who are lounging around. They are usually friendly and willing to talk of their experiences. The testaments are shipped to me from Grand Rapids, Michigan by an organization called Highway Melodies, Inc. We also insert Project Philip cards inviting people to send for Bible Studies.

We have some good responses to that. We praise the Lord for this opportunity to spread the Word and for the young married couple in our Church who pay for the Testaments! This relieves me from having to raise funds by going to local churches. I have been visiting "The Little Sisters of the Poor" care center for the elderly, which is run by the Roman Catholic Sisters. I enjoy ministering to the residents, especially the Navajo people to whom I read the Scriptures in the Navajo language. Benny Catron reads with me almost every week. He is asked to open with prayer in the Navajo language in the dining room and in the chapel service.

**Kruis Family (1994)**
**Anna next Richard & Mae Kruis (front row)**
**Ed, Dan, Bob, Brian, Rick, Philip & Ron (back row)**

# MISSIONARY'S DAUGHTER

by Anna (Sally) Kruis
*[Counsellor & Teaching Counseling; Cuba, NM]*

Whenever I tell people I grew up on the Navajo Reservation, they're impressed. They say things like, "How exciting!" or "That must've been so interesting."

I'm always taken aback for a moment. When we are children, whatever we grow up with, whatever is familiar, is taken as normal. It isn't until we encounter a wider world that we realize how extraordinary our circumstances may have been. And even today, sometimes, it is only with effort that I separate out those early experiences from who I am because they are so much a part of who I am and who I have become.

For many years I've known what a gift it was to grow up where I did, although when I was a child and adolescent I was often much more aware of how the experience seemed to be limiting me. It was a gift to be the guest of a culture so different from that of mainstream America—to play with my friends at building miniature Navajo sheep camps in the arroyo bottoms, to herd sheep with them, to race around the sheep dip on our bicycles on dipping day, to eat Navajo cake made in the earth for celebrating when a girl becomes a woman, to learn to slap and pull and pat the round, fluffy, golden fry bread, to watch the women butcher a sheep and know how every part of the sheep can be prepared and eaten, to learn to weave a Navajo rug, to accept the challenge and satisfaction of learning to communicate in another language, to see the juniper brush circles made for the winter Yeiibicheii ceremony, to hear the drums and chanting on the hill at night—my summer lullabies, to wonder about the mystery in those things. What richness and diversity for a child growing up.

I learned from watching my father that there was great joy to be found in serving. I watched his passion as he preached, using images which fit the lives of The People—The Good Shepherd, The Lamb That Was Slain. I watched him come home after driving someone thirty miles over a stony, dirt road to the hospital, only to drive back with a body, wash it, build a box and say the words over the grave. I knew he was touched by the deep poverty he saw and that he felt helpless to do enough. He saw people's pain and tried to respond. That affected me in my choices to serve.

I used all those experiences to do work I have believed in—to be part of the Navajo bilingual education movement. I could use my insider-outsider knowledge to see from a different perspective from my Navajo colleagues and thus help develop a bilingual-bicultural curriculum that has been described as "cutting edge." I experienced the bittersweet acknowledgment from a well-educated Navajo friend, "You're like us. You have an identity crisis. You don't know if you're Navajo or Bilagaana." And that, too, I've been able to use in my work as therapist. I know that my Navajo clients, struggling with issues of identity and oppression, feel seen and heard by me.

Still, I am always keenly aware of being on the outside. Of belonging and not belonging. Whenever I get onto Reservation land, I feel a powerful sense of homecoming. Yet I know I can live here only as a guest, and perhaps that is as it should be. It helps me stay aware that it is not my place to effect change here.

When I get back among The People things feel familiar. They say, "She's like us. Look at the way she puts salt in her mutton stew." There is a sense of humor that I know, and something like gratitude wells up in me when we laugh that way together. I feel grateful to be allowed to serve here where I've been given so much. And there is still always an indefinable line between us. Would it be there if I knew the language fluently? I don't know. I suspect it would.

There is another side to being a missionary's daughter. It wasn't all about being exposed to another culture. It was, in many ways, about living on the crossing of two cultures— the Navajo and the Dutch, Christian Reformed. There was a strange mixture of seeing my father learn the language and be intensely interested in the culture and of knowing he fervently believed that the most sacred parts of that culture must be destroyed in order for The People to be saved. The mystery of the Yeiibicheii shelters which caught my imagination as did the Lord's Supper, and the throbbing of the drums which transported me as the gospel hymns did, were of the Evil One, and I believed that, so I felt guilty for being touched, intrigued. Eventually, the ethics of attempting to destroy parts of a culture in the name of Christ would become a conflict for me.

I first entered a wider world when I left the Reservation to go to school at the main mission, the hub of all the smaller missions, Rehoboth. I went as a boarding school student at the age of eight and endured intense loneliness and homesickness. I was placed in the dormitory for white missionaries' children and felt I would be happier in the bigger dormitory with my friends. This experience, as any experience can, has also become a gift. I am able to empathize with Navajo of my generation and older about what it was like to be cut off from their families, their ties to the Earth, their home culture. I know something of how it affects a person. Every January 24, the anniversary of the beginning of my boarding school experience, I still remember what it was like.

Part of normal development is the idealization of our parents. Certainly I was no different, idealizing my father in his role as missionary as well as in other parts of life. Joining the wider mission world, watching other missionaries, my experience lacked the mitigation of idealization. I saw people who served out of a sense of duty, rather than joy. I saw how the hardship of living year after year alone in a single room, having no real home or social life, created bitterness and how that came out in missionaries' work as meanness and prejudice. I have Navajo friends who were deeply hurt by the experience. I experienced intentional cruelty from other missionary children who themselves lived hard, painful lives and took that out on someone more vulnerable than they. I saw the missionaries' imperfections, and like any child, I was disappointed. I rarely experienced a sense of love and joy, more often a sense of judgment and severity. I had a hard time seeing how this could win people for Christ. I felt there was more room for me on the Reservation than at the mission, despite the fact that on the Reservation I am a guest.

In the years since I have left the Christian Reformed Church, I have seen it change and become more loving and joyful. I have seen the same thing happen at Rehoboth. For myself, I have found joy in all my life, and I can truthfully say, "I have learned, whatsoever state I am in, therewith to be content."

# REFLECTIONS OF A MISSIONARY'S KID

by Rick Kruis
*[Medical Doctor in Gallup, NM)*

Growing up as a son of missionary has been a very unusual experience, if measured by other people's experience. But for me it seemed like "normal life." I didn't know anything else.

What it meant for me comes easiest as a listing in a wide variety of areas:

*APPRECIATION OF CULTURAL DIVERSITY*

One thing that immediately comes to mind is fond memories of a rich exposure to a variety of experiences and cultural contrasts. Most of the children I played with other than siblings were of a different race - usually Navajo. I wasn't aware of the differences so much. They seemed to be people just like we were. It made it hard for me later in life to understand prejudice against other races. I realize now that they were more minimized and ignored in my thinking.

We weren't allowed to witness the cultural activities and ceremonies. Navajo squaw dances and sings were thought to be religious practices inspired by the devil. Sometimes these activities were within earshot of our home in Teec Nos Pos, Arizona. To this day I have never attended the Intertribal Indian Ceremonial even though it is in my home town and current home - Gallup, New Mexico.

I regret that the missionaries, on the advice of native Christians, decided to use this approach. "Are we still throwing out the baby with the bath water?" is a question

I find myself struggling with today as I work as a physician. This especially applies to teaming up with other's in addressing the problems associated with alcohol abuse and alcoholism.

Loss of cultural identity can be a cause for considerable grief. Some medicate their feelings of loss with alcohol. So I struggle with the question, "How do you achieve a balance between introducing new ideas [Good News], and sustaining that which is good and uplifting in the traditions, beliefs and rituals of all of us.

I find a more refreshing approach in the work of Don Richardson who described some of his cross cultural evangelism in New Guinea in the book, Peace Child. Richardson seeks for parallels and symbols within the cultural belief system of the peoples he is reaching out to. Using these, he integrates the message of the gospel.

This is not to diminish the years of service put in by my father or other missionaries to the Navajos. They along with their families made great sacrifices in giving their best with the training and backing that they had from the Mission Board.

It is more than loyalty that makes me say that the strongest recollection I have as I reflect on the contributions made by my father was his dedication and how deeply he loved the people he served. The lasting impression is that he had, and still has a deep caring for people, and an urgent concern that they know the story of salvation in Jesus and have an opportunity to share in the gift of Eternal Life. This deep, caring attitude has served as an infectious role model for me. I have looked within and asked myself about my own fervor and motives.

## FAMILY FUN

We look back with some humor at the Mission Board policy of paying missionaries based on how many children they had. Whether that was the cause of our large family or not, we children for the most part look back at having grown up in a large family as a blessing. Our playmates were our siblings more often than not. It made isolation in a foreign place a matter of oblivion.

While it was great for us having a large family, we sometimes wonder how our parents survived emotionally. We lived in relative poverty — something I really have never regretted. It was especially hard on Mom with Dad being out on home visits so often. In my harshest moments of criticism, in journaling about my jealousy over my father's absences because of kingdom service, I have referred to him as "being out saving the souls of the damned [double meaning intended] Navajos" when I would have liked him to be home with me.

Being a parent now, and a bit of a work addict myself, I am more forgiving and understanding. I nevertheless find myself listening to the echo of my own words and counseling myself to heed those words in seeking a balance between service to others, enjoying my family and meeting their needs.

In fact, in defense of my father, he managed to create a lot of good memories with us. He knew how to have fun and taught us to have fun and play games, and take hikes and nature walks, and other such things. Part of our isolation and poverty was being behind the rest of the world in getting television. We were spared this wonder until I was thirteen. It meant that we spent a lot of time together listening to radio or reading. It was a custom for us all to sit on the couch while Dad or Mom read to us *Smiling Hill Farm* or some other rich classic.

## SERMONS AND INTERPRETERS

Part of growing up as a missionary's kid, was listening to your dad's sermons and then sitting through another hour of translation in a language you didn't comprehend at all. As I look for the gift in this I see that, although it did not make a good listener of me, I did learn to be creative in daydreaming and tuning out what was going on around me.

There is something very special about growing up listening to your dad's sermons. Every now and then something would stick. How many other kids get this much life teaching from their fathers? I was also in a lot of the Sunday School and Vacation Bible School classes taught by him. I know some of this teaching has had a profound impact on me and my view of life. He was enthusiastic and often used excellent teaching techniques. I always enjoyed his illustrations.

## PRAYERS OF A PREACHER

My parents are prayer warriors. They didn't only pray in public and at meal times. I have walked in on them at times to find them praying. Even today, when I stop in to give them a quick hug and hello, I find them in the midst of their prayer time, in the midst of a long list of people they are interceding for. That list includes each of their children and their families daily. It is comforting to know that we are being prayed for every day.

The prayers at our supper table must have had a profound impact on me and played a role in my decision to work in the field of alcoholism. Hardly a day went by, as I was growing up that I did not hear a prayer for some family that was suffering because of someone's drinking. I must have internalized some of the sadness, frustration and pleading that was in those prayers.

Dad, I am grateful for the opportunity to reflect on these things and record my observations for the book.

Thanks

Rick Kruis

# LIFE AS A MISSIONARY'S SON

by Dan Kruis
*[Ordained Minister; Anchorage, Alaska]*

Our life on the mission field was "the hand we were dealt". I did not choose it or regret it. It was simply the life that was given to me. When we visited family in Michigan, I knew that our life was unique and I was proud of who we were. Therefore I never would have traded it for a "normal" life in Grand Rapids or in a white middle class neighborhood anywhere.

When I was going to seminary I recognized a unique ability to relate to international students. They seemed to intuitively be aware of my acceptance of them or interest in them that was different from other students. I'm not exactly sure what it was, because I had not made a conscious effort to befriend them, but simply treated them as individuals I enjoyed. I am sure that my body language showed no discomfort and their friendship was appreciated for who they were. This natural ability to relate cross-culturally with peers has been invaluable to me.

I have at times wrestled with the advantages that Navajos have in their land rights and other rights. I have at times envied them. But my Christian heritage and inheritance is far more valuable. The opportunity of living and knowing Navajo people has made for a good life. I know that it is where I want to return as soon as possible: to enjoy living with my friends and enjoying their culture and encouraging their hearts.

Thank you for being Missionary parents.

With love, Dan

# MEMORABLE EXPERIENCES OF A MISSIONARY'S KID

by Bob Kruis
*[Building Contractor; Grand Rapids, MI]*

There are very many memorable experiences that formed the person I am. I would have to write my own biography in order to really express and show what it was like growing up a missionary's kid.

.

Some not so fun memories would include having older brothers and sisters leaving home to go to boarding school and eventually my going to boarding school myself. I remember being a white student in a school class with two other white girls and the other twenty eight kids were Indians who weren't very willing to include me in what they were playing, let alone talk English so that I could understand their conversation. It wasn't always so fun to sit through your dad's sermon and then listen to it again in Navajo and the translation was never completed in less time than my father's sermon. It was a good thing my father wasn't very long winded. One of my memories included riding 13 mi. to school and back on a dirty, dusty, bumpy road every day.

The good things far out weighed the not so fun things. Even the 13 mi. bus ride was a time to meditate and ponder how the beautiful rock formations were created. I remember riding on the bumper of the pickup truck. Once we had picked up so many people that we couldn't fit them all into the back (and sometimes we just rode on the bumper for the fun of it). Living in areas where Sunday afternoon hikes could bring you to the edge of a 100 ft. cliff, or a canyon with beautiful trickling stream in the summer and cascading ice falls in the winter wasn't too hard to live with. To this day, I miss the freedom to hike just about anywhere a person would want. I can remember how proud I was of the work my parents were doing. I enjoyed telling visitors from Michigan about the Indians, the area, and about the mission post we were stationed at. I would try to tell them all I knew about the different cultures and different areas, and how I thought it was such an advantage to live where we were living.

Advantages and disadvantages aside, I always figured growing up a missionary's kid wasn't much different than any other child growing up with Christian parents. There were bullies at school, there were memory verses to learn, there were chores to do and homework I didn't like to do. But there were also games with mom and dad to be played. There were hikes to go on, fishing trips at four in the morning with dad, camping trips, trips to Michigan, ice skating, and many other fun activities.

Mixed in with the fun and the not so fun, mom and dad were always a constant witness and a good example for me. I can remember dad once said something like, " I hope and pray that I will be instrumental in leading all my children to the Lord. " This caused me to think of a sermon dad preached about Rahab the harlot. I thought if God could use a woman like Rahab to save his spies and eventually have Christ born as her descendant, God could love and use me too, even though I had become a thief ( I was stealing money from mom and dad's tithe container). Through that sermon God spoke to me, and I decided to give my life to Jesus. I would have to say this was the greatest advantage of all in my life in being raised a missionary's child.

# GROWING UP AS A MISSIONARY'S CHILD

by Ed Kruis
*[Theater Set & Lighting Designer, Counselling Student;*
*Las Cruces, NM]*

One of the best parts of being a child of a missionary was being raised in beautiful Northern New Mexico. I smile when I think of the number of times I've heard people speak of New Mexico as a barren wasteland and I feel bad for them because they have not learned to see the beauty that I've enjoyed. What some have chosen to call barren, I prefer to call stark. The landscape of mesas, rocks, forests, solitary trees upon a savannah of sagebrush present harsh and dynamic contrasts accented by crystalline sunlight. And for me there is no way to accurately describe the smell of New Mexico after a rain; the mixture of pungent sage and juniper and the earthy aroma of that heavy clay that clings in increasing wads to the boots of any who braves the field after a rain.

Our backyard and playground for many years was the wilderness of the Navajo Nation. We spent Summers swimming and fishing in small reservoirs and building dams in canyons to make swimming holes. We spent years just climbing rocks and hiking through mountains and canyons. One of my favorite memories is of the sack lunches mom would make for us to take out to a rock and eat.

Another of the best of being a missionary kid was the Navajo people. I will never forget people like grandpa Talley and Mary Havens, of Tohlakai, whose welcoming smile is for me the epitome of Navajo graciousness and hospitality. My first chums in elementary school were Duane and Timothy Yazzie and Wallace Curley. For the first four years of school, we were inseparable.

From all of these people I learned bits and pieces of the Navajo language and culture. Yet while I never became fluent in either, I learned a great love for language, and to celebrate the diversity of God's rich creation and different peoples.

One of the hardest parts of being a missionary kid was being uprooted every so often to adjust to a new home, new school and new friends. The positive side of this was strength of bonds between family members. Still, to this day, it is difficult to stay in one place for very long before I feel some urgency to move along.

Another difficult aspect was that I was often a minority in the classroom while representing the majority culture. I felt I was in a "no-mans" land and did what I could to fit in. I don't know that it was so much an issue of cultural differences, though I'm sure that had some influence. It was more a matter of accepting and acceptance.

All in all, though my childhood was not mainstream America, the dynamics of growing up was not, from my point of view all that different from most everyone.

Ed Kruis

# ABOUT BEING A
# MISSIONARY'S CHILD

by Ron Kruis
*[Dean of Students; Rehoboth Christian School; Rehoboth, NM]*

My thoughts and feelings about being a child of a missionary are bittersweet. Although, my bitter experiences turned out to have their rewards later in life.

The sweet memories were many. The beautiful country that we were honored to grow in will forever be in my blood. I enjoyed living with my family on the reservation, hiking in the mountains and canyons. I also loved the times I could be with Dad on camp work. I remember feeding a lamb beside a hogan when I was a pre-schooler and an elderly Navajo woman standing by laughing. I will always have respect for the Navajo grandma. I have made many other Navajo friends.

The bitter side had to do with getting along with another culture. Up until about the 10th grade I was often picked on by Navajo children. I was laughed at and sometimes hit or chased. I was misunderstood, but those trials taught me patience and compassion. It taught me to make an extra effort to get along with those around me.

We wore clothes from the missionary barrel, yet we always had food on the table and learned that material possessions do not make us happy or any more faithful to God.

I have great memories of my childhood and would not trade with anyone. I have much respect for my parents, they went through many difficult times for the sake of the gospel, their nine children and the Navajo. I praise God for them.

# GROWING UP AS A MISSIONARY'S SON

by Philip Kruis
*[Assistant Pastor & Counsellor; Tucson, AZ]*

What it was like for me growing up as a missionary's son:

One of my first memories is going on a visit with my father in the old green Ford pickup he had at the time. As was my father's natural bent, we were traveling rather fast over the rutted and rough dirt road. With little warning and great surprise, we dove into a washout in the road with such a great impact that my face slammed into the dashboard causing me to howl with pain as the crimson flow from my nose soaked my shirt. Dad gently helped me stop the bleeding and my tears and then continued his trip, his mind set on the task before him – the planting or watering of the seed of the gospel or perhaps harvesting the fruit of a ripened faith.

Dad and Mom's lives were living examples for me to see how precious the gospel was. The extent of their sacrifice ranged from giving up a life-style of material wealth and riches to picking up hitchhikers or giving someone in need a meal or a place to lay their head. Their acts of kindness were not done with boastful or proud hearts but with a desire to serve others and share God's blessings. In doing so they have touched many lives and without a doubt one most powerfully touched was mine. I've heard it said that parents teach by example. This was certainly true of Mom and Dad. Their lives are living testimonies – teaching the grace of God and the love of Christ to me, a sinner saved by that amazing grace.

We never had much in the world's eyes but we had all we needed and then some in God's eyes. "To grow up a missionary's son", some would say, "must have been difficult". I would have had it no other way.

Philip.

# FINDING FULFILLMENT AS A MISSIONARY'S SON

by Brian Kruis
*[Christian School Principal; Zuni, NM]*

"Do you love Jesus? Do you believe that He died for your sins? Do you want to follow Him?" I heard these questions often as I grew up and now as an adult, they ring out urgently from my heart to a world that needs hope and salvation. These questions probably made the biggest impact on my life as the child of missionary parents. Dad and Mom didn't just share the Good News with the Navahos, they also evangelized and discipled our family The most important thing for Dad and Mom has been that we and others serve and love Jesus and find our fulfillment in Him.

It wasn't always easy being a missionary child. I remember feelings of jealousy and anger when our lives had to be shared with anyone who showed up at the door. It didn't matter if it was our birthday or a holiday or meal time or late at night. People who needed help would not be turned away. Our lives would become a part of theirs so that we could share the love of Jesus. While it wasn't always easy, Dad and Mom showed us what it meant to be servants and God blessed our lives.

I feel that God has blessed my life by allowing me to grow up experiencing so much from the Native American culture. Some people may think that it would not be good to raise children up on the reservation, but I feel that my family has been richly blessed by the experiences that we have had. We have all been challenged to make the most of the abilities God has given us in service to Him.

For the last 10 years as I have been working on the Zuni Indian reservation, sharing the Good News about Jesus, I have been thankful for their prayers and encouragement and their steadfastness in their faith in Jesus.

# That They Might Know

### Remembrances of a Christian Southwest Missionary

### by *Missionary Richard Kruis*

*First Edition Publication — August, 1995*

Mail Order Form To: **Richard Kruis; 221 Verdi Dr., Gallup, NM 87301**

**Name:** _____

**Address:**_____

**Phone:** _____

**City** _____ **State** ___ **Zip** _____

**Number of Copies:** _____

**Soft cover $9.95** *Please add $2.00 shipping costs*

**Amount Enclosed:** _____